NATURAL RESOURCES

NATURAL RESOURCES
Bureaucratic Myths and Environmental Management

By
RICHARD L. STROUP AND JOHN A. BADEN
With the assistance of
DAVID T. FRACTOR

Foreword by
WILLIAM A. NISKANEN

Pacific Studies in Public Policy

PACIFIC INSTITUTE FOR PUBLIC POLICY RESEARCH
San Francisco, California

Ballinger Publishing Company
Cambridge, Massachusetts
A Subsidiary of Harper & Row, Publishers, Inc.

International Standard Book Number: 0-88410-380-3 (CL)
0-88410-385-4 (PB)

Library of Congress Catalog Card Number: 83-2607

Printed in the United States of America

Library of Congress Cataloging in Publication Data

Stroup, Richard.
    Natural resources.

    (Pacific studies in public policy)
    Bibliography: p.
    Includes index.
    1. Conservation of natural resources—United States—Decision making. 2. Conservation of natural resources—Government policy—United States. 3. Environmental protection—United States—Decision making. 4. Environmental policy—United States.
    I. Baden, John. II. Fractor, David T. III. Title. IV. Series.
    HC103.7.S84   1983   333.7'0973   83-2607
    ISBN 0-88410-380-3 (Ballinger)
    ISBN 0-88410-385-4 (Ballinger : pbk.)

PACIFIC INSTITUTE
FOR PUBLIC POLICY RESEARCH

The Pacific Institute for Public Policy Research is an independent, tax-exempt research and educational organization. The Institute's program is designed to broaden public understanding of the nature and effects of market processes and government policy.

With the bureaucratization and politicization of modern society, scholars, business and civic leaders, the media, policymakers, and the general public have too often been isolated from meaningful solutions to critical public issues. To facilitate a more active and enlightened discussion of such issues, the Pacific Institute sponsors in-depth studies into the nature and possible solutions to major social, economic, and environmental problems. Undertaken regardless of the sanctity of any particular government program, or the customs, prejudices, or temper of the times, the Institute's studies aim to ensure that alternative approaches to currently problematic policy areas are fully evaluated, the best remedies discovered, and these findings made widely available. The results of this work are published as books and monographs, and form the basis for numerous conference and media programs.

Through this program of research and commentary, the Institute seeks to evaluate the premises and consequences of government policy, and provide the foundations necessary for constructive policy reform.

FORTHCOMING

Politics, Prices, and Petroleum
A Study in the Political Economy of Energy

Inflation or Deflation?
Capital Formation, Employment, and the Economy

The American Family and the State

Forestlands
Public and Private

Urban Transit
Public Failure and Private Renaissance

Rationing Health Care
Medical Licensing in the United States

New Strategies for American Unions
The Economic Consequences

Free to Close
The Economics and Politics of Plant Closings

Electric Utility Regulation and the Energy Crisis

For further information on the Pacific Institute's program and a catalogue of publications, please contact:

PACIFIC INSTITUTE
FOR PUBLIC POLICY RESEARCH
635 Mason Street
San Francisco, California 94108

PACIFIC STUDIES IN PUBLIC POLICY

Locking Up the Range
Federal Land Controls and Grazing
By Gary D. Libecap
With a Foreword by Jonathan R. T. Hughes

The Public School Monopoly
A Critical Analysis of Education and the State
in American Society
Edited by Robert B. Everhart
With a Foreword by Clarence J. Karier

Resolving the Housing Crisis
Government Policy, Decontrol, and the Public Interest
Edited with an Introduction by M. Bruce Johnson

Water Rights
Scarce Resource Allocation, Bureaucracy, and
the Environment
Edited with an Introduction by Terry L. Anderson
With a Foreword by Jack Hirshleifer

Firearms and Violence
Issues of Public Policy
Edited by Don B. Kates, Jr.
With a Foreword by John Kaplan

Rights and Regulation
Ethical, Political, and Economic Issues
Edited by Tibor M. Machan and M. Bruce Johnson
With a Foreword by Aaron Wildavsky

CONTENTS

FOREWORD

For scholars and the general public alike, this book is probably the best available one on the economics of natural resources and the environment. An impressive range of resource management issues is addressed, including energy, minerals, wildlife, grazing, forestry, groundwater, and air and water pollution. The book focuses on the many innocent-sounding myths that have often plagued public discussion of these issues and confronts misconceptions with the realities of both private and public resource management.

As its central theme, the book argues that the management of natural resources is primarily affected by the structure of the property rights of the effective manager (public or private). In each case, the authors suggest changes in these property rights that would increase the sum of the net benefits to the affected parties. The writing is clear, concise, and interesting. A careful reader will also learn a lot of economics as a by-product, without wading through the graphs and equations that so often limit the communications of contemporary economists.

The book may induce the reader to question why the general solutions to these resource issues have not already been accepted. The answer is that economists have too often avoided the central *political* issue. A solution that increases the sum of the net benefits does not necessarily increase the net benefits to each affected party. Most people, however, are more concerned about the expected net benefits to their own group and have little interest in general efficiency.

Critics may find that, in this sense, the book is incomplete. The initial distribution of property rights *is* important, primarily as it affects the potential for a consensus for change. For example, the authors promote the superiority of an effluent tax on stationary-source pollution. In this case, it is likely that the distribution of marketable permits to existing polluters will be more acceptable to all affected parties. In addition, since market transactions are not costless, some care in the initial distribution of rights can reduce the expected future transaction costs.

The major remaining challenge is to design solutions that are efficient to *each* affected party. The lessons of this book should stimulate readers to exercise their own creativity on how to structure such solutions. The final test of whether a change in resource management would be efficient is not the consensus of economists but the consensus of the affected parties.

William A. Niskanen
Member, President's Council of Economic Advisers
Washington, D.C.

PREFACE

Rising demands for natural resources and a seemingly endless supply of horror stories regarding resource exploitation continue to make natural-resource decision making a prime arena for policy debate — if not open warfare — among special interest groups. Fears of material shortages and environmental disaster are common, and the potential and limitations of both private- and public-sector resource management are widely misunderstood. Mythology is rampant in discussions of these issues. This volume is intended to provide some insights and to increase the reader's understanding of the issues surrounding the management of natural resources and the alternatives that are available.

We have been influenced in our writing by authors too numerous to mention in the neoclassical, property rights, public choice, and Austrian traditions. We gratefully acknowledge extensive contributions at many stages of our work from Terry Anderson, Charles Baird, B. Delworth Gardner, P. J. Hill, M. Bruce Johnson, Ron Johnson, and William Siffin. This book benefited greatly from the assistance of Tanya Cameron, David Fractor, Michael Hetherington, and JoAnn McDonald. We owe a special debt of gratitude to Marianne Keddington, Lynn Scarlett, and Alan Hislop for their editorial assistance. Each of these people in his or her own way was vital to the work and its exposition. None had the final approval rights that would permit us to share the blame for any remaining problems.

We particularly want to extend our appreciation to the Pacific Institute for Public Policy Research and its President, David Theroux, for his suggestions in formulating and steering the book through its various stages, and for the opportunity to build, exchange, and refine many of the ideas contained in this volume.

Richard Stroup
John Baden

Chapter 1
AMERICA IN THE 1980s
Continuing the Noble Experiment

As the United States enters the mid-1980s and approaches the bicentennial of the Constitution (ratified in 1789), the mood of the nation is best described as apprehensive. Americans are understandably concerned about an economy marked by inflation and high unemployment, a deteriorating natural environment, shortages of some natural resources and escalating prices of many others, diminished national security, declining productivity resulting in decreased standards of living, and significant diminution in individual freedom.

Under existing institutions these apprehensions are well founded indeed. Fortunately, if we review our constitutional foundations, we find that these outcomes are not inevitable, popular predictions of doom notwithstanding. The United States was consciously conceived as an experimental social institution. In effect, this country has served as a social laboratory for nearly two hundred years, and it is important that experimentation continue.

In this volume, we observe data from the experiment and draw conclusions from them. The result is a fundamental theme: Individual freedom, high productivity, and environmental quality are not necessarily antagonistic. Indeed, under specified institutional arrangements these characteristics are reinforcing. When aggregated, they yield increasing social welfare and enhanced environmental quality. The process is complicated, however, by a number of factors.

Natural resources are found in technically complex, highly inter-dependent systems. At the same time, these systems are often loaded with heavy emotional baggage. The conjunction of technical complexity and high emotion tends to inhibit careful and dispassionate analysis, yet it is exactly this sort of analysis that is needed to promote the kind of resource management that leads to high social welfare.

Because of the complexity of natural systems, general understanding of them tends to be extremely limited. While most people may be emotionally neutral toward most important human artifacts, many have very strong beliefs and preferences regarding wildlife, forests, grasslands, and bodies of water. The combination of inadequate information and high emotions offers a fertile breeding ground for many misconceptions about the appropriate management of natural resources. The roles played by private property rights, the profit motive, bureaucracy, and bureaucrats are all commonly misunderstood, and each has been falsely blamed for serious problems. Public discussion of these problems has produced a lot of heat but very little light.

In response to this muddled and sometimes vehement discussion of natural resource problems, we propose to review and dissect the misconceptions or misguided beliefs that surround natural resource management. Second, we shall describe the relevant properties of the policies and resource systems addressed. Finally, we shall demonstrate how a system of property rights and market exchange can lead to improvements in efficiency and, perhaps, in equity. We do not, of course, advocate a particular standard of equity; rather, we attempt to explain the efficiency and the equity implications of alternative institutional arrangements.

It is important to remember that we are considering resource systems in a nation—the United States—that operates with an avowedly experimental system. This system is peculiar in the most precise sense of that much abused term: When measured against modal patterns of societies, the system is eccentric, distinctive, particular, and unique. Obviously, when described in infinite detail, any structure more complex than an atom is unique. But we mean more than that.

The development of the U.S. Constitution is one of the intellectual highlights of human history. Since the time of the ancients, it has been widely understood that government, with its monopoly on sanctified coercion, has the potential for being the most efficient engine ever designed for the generation of plunder. Government is able to engineer huge wealth transfers with a minimum of violence. There is, naturally, competition for control of that exploitative potential. Thus, in all societies at all times political power and economic power show a positive correlation. Individuals who have one usually have the other as well. In most systems, the best investment available to individuals is in the political process. By influencing government, one can influence the distribution of wealth. It is no surprise, then, that political activity in general is oriented toward transfer activities.

The fundamental and distinctive characteristic of the U. S. Constitution has been its emphasis on rewarding the creation of wealth, or *productive* activity, relative to *transfer* activity. The Constitution was written to protect the freedom of contract and to restrict the activities of the federal government. Under this system, individuals gain by doing what others desire most; they do well for themselves when they do good for others. It is interesting that the Declaration of Independence and the *Wealth of Nations* were published in the same year. Both Adam Smith and the authors of the Constitution understood the importance of fostering exchange on the basis of willing consent. They also understood that there are dangers inherent in relaxing the rules of willing consent and relying on the legalized coercion of the governmental apparatus. The Constitution made it more difficult in the United States, compared with other nations, to take the property (wealth) of a citizen without getting his willing consent through exchange.

The following chapters demonstrate the relevance of this admittedly sketchy detour into political history and social philosophy. The U. S. Constitution was established to foster individual freedom and to promote the general welfare by encouraging the movement of resources to more highly valued uses. Natural resources are fundamental components of human welfare. In terms of general social welfare, it is unfortunate that our natural resources are allocated more and more by the political process. By moving toward political allocation and away from the rule of willing consent, we have moved from a society that rewards productive activity and willing exchange to one where many of a person's best investment opportunities lie in influencing transfer activities. In the material that follows, we will examine this movement and propose positive policy changes that can improve our circumstances.

In order to develop effective policy formulation, we must predict human behavior and reaction, and successful prediction requires effective social science. Microeconomics, the science of individual decision making, is the one social science capable of making consistently accurate predictions regarding the outcomes of policy alternatives.

People are not like the entities studied by physical scientists. People have purposes, make conscious decisions, and learn from experience. Their actions are not governed simply by the laws of physics and chemistry. People perceive, reason, and are influenced by emotion. As a result, social science is complex and imprecise. Yet, it is useful because human behavior is not random; it is partially predictable.

Our microeconomic approach to natural resource management and to the prediction of policy outcomes begins with eight assumptions.

1. Individuals, on average, are predominantly self-interested. This is not to suggest that altruism is as rare as unicorns. Altruism certainly exists. To assert that individuals are primarily motivated by self-interest merely suggests that when individuals evaluate the projected impact of an action, their first question is, "How will that action affect the things I value?" Obviously, the welfare of others, especially relatives and friends, is often included in the calculation; but self-interest influences any decision maker's perception of a given problem, as well as possible alternatives, and of his selection of a solution.

2. The provision of a scarce good implies a cost or a trade-off. In other words, apart from increases in efficiency, "there is no such thing as a free lunch." For example, to have a congressionally designated wilderness area, a "free good," we give up the opportunity for development. Although trading off wilderness against development is often worthwhile, depending on tastes and preferences, there is nevertheless a cost.

3. Decision makers economize on the resources over which they have both control and responsibility. This follows from the fact that they act purposefully. In general, decision makers select those options that they believe will advance their own welfare. Thus, the preferences of individuals are revealed by the choices they make.

4. Human choice is significantly influenced by incentives. This is a fundamental law of economics. As the costs to an individual of

choosing a particular option increase, that option is less likely to be selected. This principle, the first law of demand, approaches in verity the fundamental laws of physical science.

5. Individuals are sensitive to relative shifts in the costs and benefits of competing alternatives. Thus, humans consistently seek substitutes in terms of products and activities that will yield higher net satisfaction. Individuals are also sensitive to increments in costs and benefits. This is commonly referred to as the "marginal" principle of economics. For example, the marginal cost of producing or consuming a good is defined as the cost associated with an *incremental* unit. We can expect the added unit to be produced if the cost *to the decision maker* is less than the added benefit to him.

6. It is rational for individuals to obtain less than complete information before making a decision. Like other resources, information is scarce, and something must be given up—time, effort, or money— to obtain more of it. Thus, intelligent decision makers will not normally obtain perfect or even state-of-the-art knowledge about the future. Rational decision makers are expected to stop investing in additional information when its expected value equals the cost of obtaining it. We can expect the sensible voter or consumer to conserve on efforts to obtain increments of information just as he conserves on other scarce resources.

7. Ecological and economic systems share a fundamental characteristic. The most basic law of ecology states that everything is interrelated: It is impossible to do just one thing. This "law" also characterizes economic systems. Actions have effects beyond those intended.

8. The kind of rationing system imposed can have a large impact on the amount there is to ration. Scarcity has always been an important aspect of all systems because, most simply, human wants always exceed availabilities. This implies that there must be a rationing system in all societies. From the standpoint of general social welfare, the best rationing system fosters the movement of resources to more highly valued uses and provides those resources to those who value them most. Any alternative that violates this standard is socially inefficient.

An understanding of these eight assumptions and their applications can be productive when evaluating natural resource policy. In general, public-spirited actions regarding environmental quality, resource management, and other public issues have tended to be oriented rather simplistically toward desired outcomes rather than toward processes carefully designed to produce those outcomes. Good intentions are just not sufficient; the processes are critical. To quote from Pacific Institute Research Director Bruce Johnson:

> Processes are . . . critical to producing desired results. Since the economic and political landscape is littered with the wreckage of well-intentioned but disappointing programs, the thoughtful activist cannot ignore the economists' warnings. Government environmental protection programs have not fulfilled their positive promises on the one hand and have led to unanticipated negative consequences on the other. . . . Enough evidence is now available to suggest that the resulting frustration cannot be eliminated by means of "better" programs with "better" people running them. . . . More attention should be devoted to the processes that led to the original, undesirable outcome as well as to the processes set in motion when we adopt new programs to solve the problems.[1]

The political economy model presented in this volume can aid in an understanding of the processes that will lead to efficient resource management, enhanced social welfare, and greater individual freedom. Pessimism is not only depressing, it is also unnecessary and dysfunctional. When the prevailing institutions align personal responsibility more closely with authority over resource allocation, good things begin to happen. Waste, bypassed opportunities, and the unjustified sacrifice of environmental values can be powerfully discouraged. The potential for improving our circumstances and dissipating apprehension clearly exists. This volume continues our efforts to achieve these goals.

---

1. John Baden and Richard L. Stroup, eds., *Bureaucracy vs. Environment* (Ann Arbor: University of Michigan Press, 1981), p. 218.

Chapter 2

PROPERTY RIGHTS

The Real Issue

Property rights to a resource, whether a tract of land, a coal mine, or a spring creek, consist of having control over that resource. Such rights are most valuable when ownership is outright and when property can be easily exchanged for other goods and services. Although an important feature of a property right is the power to exclude others from using it, even limited command over access to a resource confers status and power to the holder. Governments typically exercise at least some discretionary command in this regard.[1] As Douglass North wrote, "One cannot develop a useful analysis of the state divorced from property rights."[2] Indeed, a theory of property rights can become a theory of the state.

It is a common misconception that every citizen benefits from his share of the public lands and the resources found thereon. Public ownership of many natural resources lies at the root of resource control conflicts. With public ownership resources are held in common; that is, they are owned by everyone and, therefore, can be used by everyone. But public ownership by no means guarantees public ben-

1. See Robert Dorfman, "The Technical Basis for Decision Making," in *The Governance of Common Property Resources*, ed. Edwin T. Haefele (Baltimore: Johns Hopkins University Press, 1974); and Richard Stroup and John Baden, "Property Rights and Natural Resource Management," *Literature of Liberty* (October–December 1979), pp. 5–17.
2. Douglass North, "A Framework for Analyzing the State in Economic History," *Explorations in Economic History* 16 (1979): 250.

efits. Individuals make decisions regarding resource use, not large groups or societies. Yet, with government control, it is not the owners who make decisions, but politicians and bureaucrats. The citizen as beneficiary is often a fiction.

It is useful to characterize an institutional arrangement by describing how it defines and defends property rights and makes them transferable. Over the past few years, economists and others have developed a property rights paradigm that examines these institutional characteristics, making it possible to analyze events based on actual or proposed institutional changes.

The property rights paradigm provides important analytical leverage that is useful for understanding how individuals interact in institutional contexts. The paradigm helps us to understand history, to predict the consequences of modern institutions, and to compare the likely outcomes of alternative arrangements. Given the growing pressures from larger populations and from technologies that enable us to acquire and process more natural resources, such predictive and analytical capabilities take on increasing importance. We *must* manage with care. The costs of failure are increasing.

PROPERTY RIGHTS AND ALLOCATION OF RESOURCES

Most economists begin their analyses by assuming that decision makers seek to maximize profits, income, or even wealth. Property rights theorists assume that the decision maker's goals or utility function must first be specified in each case. It is assumed that the decision maker will maximize his own utility—not that of some institution or state—in whatever situation he finds himself.[3]

Individuals seek their own advantage within prevailing institutional arrangements. Nevertheless, they may attempt to change the "rules of the game" or the institutions themselves. When privately held property rights to urban land are attenuated by building height restrictions, for example, landowners may gain by changing the rules or by influencing their administration. Since others will fight these changes or seek similar advantages for themselves, the resulting com-

3. For an excellent review, see Eirik Furubotn and Svetozar Pejovich, "Property Rights and Economic Theory: A Survey of Recent Literature," *Journal of Economic Literature* 10 (1972): 1137–62.

petition may be a negative sum game. In such economic situations, the winners gain less than the losses suffered or investments made by their competitors.[4] In effect, then, negative sum games result in a net economic loss to society.

Institutional rules always allow governmental officials some discretion in determining access to resources. Claimants, therefore, have an incentive to invest in activities that might produce administrative outcomes favorable to themselves. Under these circumstances, some corruption exists in every political system. Informational lobbying, potential shifts of campaign support, actual or threatened lawsuits, and even bribery can all be brought to bear—at a cost—by those who wish to gain favorable decisions from governmental policymakers who control the rights to resources.

Economic growth and efficiency are greatly affected by the way in which existing institutions allow property rights to be traded and allocated.[5] When rights are both privately held and easily transferable, decision makers have easy access to information through bid and asked prices, as well as an incentive to move resources to higher valued uses. But if a person can gain by blocking socially useful resource moves through governmental means, then his gain is society's loss. Similarly, if potential users can gain access to the resource through government without paying the opportunity costs of the resource, then low-valued uses may dominate at the expense of more highly valued uses.

THE EVOLUTION OF PROPERTY RIGHTS TO NATURAL RESOURCES

In analyzing the effects of alternative institutional arrangements for resource allocation, it is useful to look at the evolution of those institutions that established and protected property rights to natural resources. As part of that effort, an examination of the western

---

4. See Anne O. Krueger, "The Political Economy of the Rent Seeking Society," *American Economic Review* 64 (June 1974): 291–303; and Gordon Tullock, "The Welfare Costs of Tariffs, Monopolies, and Theft," *Western Economic Journal* 5 (June 1967): 224–32.
5. See, for example, Steven N. S. Cheung, "The Structure of a Contract and the Theory of a Non-Exclusive Resource," *Journal of Law and Economics* 13 (April 1970): 49–70; Harold Demsetz, "Toward a Theory of Property Rights," *American Economic Review* 57 (May 1967): 347–59; and Furubotn and Pejovich, "Property Rights and Economic Theory."

American frontier allows us to compare methods of defining and enforcing these property rights.[6] Two basic themes in the evolution of natural resource property rights emerge from a reading of *The Frontier in American History* by Frederick Jackson Turner.[7] First, American institutions were formed as pioneers ventured into the West and resource constraints changed. Second, opportunities provided by the frontier placed a lower limit on wages. In a general way, these observations help explain how property rights evolved as a response to changing resource prices.

We can theorize that as more information was obtained about natural resources and as their value rose, potential rents to the resources induced decision makers to develop them and thus to define and enforce the property rights governing them. Further, when voluntary associations of resource users developed and enforced these rights, a strong incentive arose to allocate the resource efficiently. Finally, as the geographic frontier closed and the number of unclaimed resources declined, individual options for increasing wealth became limited to increasing productivity, confiscating resources through legitimate or illegitimate means, or both.

History of Frontier Development

The western American frontier in the late eighteenth century contained abundant natural resources with virtually no institutions or conventions to govern their use. As long as the expected value of the marginal product of labor combined with frontier resources was less than the opportunity cost of labor in other areas, the frontier resources were not exploited. But as the demand for outputs produced from natural resources increased and the opportunity cost of employing those resources fell, settlers moved to the frontier.

When free to choose their own process for defining property rights, settlers had incentives to reduce bargaining costs. Because native American claims to resources often were not enforced by the government, their conflicts with white settlers over the control

---

6. For a more detailed account, see Terry L. Anderson and Peter J. Hill, "Property Rights as a Common Pool Resource," in *Bureaucracy vs. Environment*, ed. John Baden and Richard Stroup (Ann Arbor: University of Michigan Press, 1981), pp. 22–43.

7. Frederick Jackson Turner, *The Frontier in American History* (New York: Krieger, 1920), p. 343.

of land were settled by force. Though this was a rather expensive activity, there generally remained a strong incentive to economize in property rights definition.

Actual or potential owners have incentives to use their resources efficiently. In contrast, agents with no stake in the residuals of the bargaining process (e.g., a bureaucrat at the Environmental Protection Agency [EPA] or the attorney in a divorce suit) have no direct and personal interest in reducing the cost of that process. Of course, when such third parties are easily monitored *and* there is competition for their jobs, incentives do appear, but this seldom occurs in the public sector. On the American frontier, the first efforts to settle resource allocation claims emerged through the establishment of voluntary associations and the development of informal property rights to resources. Land clubs, claims associations, cattlemen's associations, wagon trains, and mining camps within which individuals grappled with the allocation of water, land, livestock, minerals, timber, and even personal property all represent attempts to mitigate the problems associated with common ownership.

The forms of voluntary association varied, but each sought to bring order to competing multiple claims before the formal claims process applied to the land. These groups often had bylaws, a constitution, a management pact, a leadership selection process, and a procedure for handling disputes. In addition, outsiders who attempted to interfere with a claim held by a member of the group were confronted by the association's considerable enforcement power.

> From successive frontiers of our American history have developed needed customs, laws and organizations. The era of fur-trading produced its hunters, its barter, and the great fur companies; on the mining frontier came the staked claims and the vigilante committees; the camp meeting and the circuit rider were heard on the religious outposts; on the margins of settlement the claims clubs protected the rights of the squatter farmers; on the ranchmen's frontier the millions of cattle, the vast ranches, and the cattle companies produced pools and local, district, territorial, and national cattle associations.[8]

This process of defining individual property rights resulted in relatively low-cost methods. Claims associations in Iowa, for example, required that their members contribute from zero to fifty dollars in value each six months the claim was held. Likewise, cattlemen and livestock associations throughout the West sought to define and en-

8. Louis Pelzer, *The Cattlemen's Frontier* (Glendale, Calif.: Russell Sage, 1936), p. 87.

force property rights while conserving the resources necessary to the definition and enforcement process.

Two basic institutional methods were used to allocate property rights to the vast frontier resources: (1) "squatter sovereignty," or preemption, and (2) the acquisition of water rights. Typically, simple settlement was sufficient to enforce squatters' claims since the abundance of natural resources reduced the seeds of conflict. Later, however, range rights were established through crude advertising and were enforced by livestock associations. Water rights as a claims method typically entailed homesteading adjacent to water or filing claims where state or territorial laws prevailed.

Throughout this period, these extralegal, voluntary associations economized on definition and enforcement techniques. They recognized that high bargaining costs consumed resources that they intuitively knew could be put to better use.

The Frontiersman versus the Law

The Easterner, with his background of forest and farm, could not always understand the man of the cattle kingdom. One went on foot, the other went on horseback; one carried his law in books, the other carried his strapped around his waist. One represented tradition, the other represented innovation; one responded to convention, the other responded to necessity and evolved his own conventions. Yet the man of the timber and the town made the law for the man of the plain; the plainsman, finding this law unsuited to his needs, broke it and was called lawless.[9]

In the late nineteenth century, as statutory mandates dating from 1785 focused on the rapid disposition and transfer of government lands to private parties and the promotion of the family farm, the growing conservation movement began charging private enterprise and private ownership with exploitation. The movement to preserve the public lands intensified.

To the extent that initial disposal schemes recognized scarcities, efficiencies were realized. But the change in policy evidenced by the Homestead Act of 1862 reversed eight decades of relatively unfettered land disposal and minimal transaction costs by requiring often economically unrealistic labor and capital expenditures to retain land

---

9. Walter Prescott Webb, *The Great Plains* (Boston: Grosset and Dunlap, 1931), p. 206.

ownership. This reversal, of course, produced economic inefficiency, considerable human suffering, and even death.

As third party agents, the government increasingly interfered in resource allocations, setting the stage for the blossoming and growth of transfer activity. It is this institutional setting, now matured, that dominates property rights considerations in natural resource development, allocation, sale, and preservation.

The Growth of Transfer Activity

When the rule of willing consent applies, the transfer (exchange) of property is expected to benefit both parties. In contrast, when the coercive power of government is employed to transfer property from one party to another, neither equity nor efficiency can be assumed. It was these politically determined transfers that disturbed Sitting Bull—with serious consequences for Custer and his party. Politically enforced transfers require the use of the coercive power of government to transfer rights from one individual or group to another.[10] Since individual wealth is a direct function of the property rights held, an institutional environment that allows coercive transfer activity will greatly increase the marginal benefit of using resources to generate transfers.

The closing of the American frontier compounded the effect of increased returns from transfer activity. Whereas the frontier had permitted individuals to increase their wealth by establishing property rights to previously unclaimed resources, the closing of the frontier enhanced the benefits to be gained from expending resources for transfer activity. This is not the zero sum game claimed by many economists—that one's gain must come at a loss to another—but rather a negative sum game in which the resources spent by some in generating and by others in opposing transfer activity lead to a *net* loss. The private gain of one is more than offset by the other's loss coupled with the unproductive waste of resources used in the process.

Beginning with the Slaughterhouse cases (1873) and continuing through *Munn* v. *Illinois* (1877) and *Muller* v. *Oregon* (1908), the institutional setting of property rights definition began to change.

10. For more information, see Terry Anderson and Peter J. Hill, *The Birth of a Transfer Society* (Stanford, Calif.: Hoover Institution Press, 1980).

Third parties were increasingly granted a "property right" in what had previously been another's exclusive resource. This historical foundation provides the context within which conflicts over the definition of current property rights regarding natural resources can be judged.

RIGHTS, MARKETS, AND RESOURCE MANAGEMENT

Another common but mistaken belief is that without social regulation, resources will be managed for profit, not people. When a natural resource is privately owned, it is often thought that the owner has only his conscience to tell him to pay attention to the desires of others. Normally, however, it is the *absence* of private, transferble ownership that leads to the resource user's lack of concern for others' desires. Private ownership holds the individual owner responsible for allocating a resource to its highest valued use, whether or not the resource is used by others. If the buffalo is not mine until I kill it and I cannot sell my interest in the living animal to another, I have no incentive – beyond altruism – to investigate others' interest in it. I will do with it as I wish. But if the buffalo is mine and I may sell it, I am motivated to consider others' value estimates of the animal. I will misuse the buffalo only at my economic peril.[11] How does this work?

Privately owned resources that are freely transferable generate decentralized decisions regarding resource uses. The market rations scarce resources and coordinates individual plans. For example, the owner of a copper mine receives information on the value of alternative uses, as well as the incentive to supply the highest valued use, through bids for copper ore or offers to buy the mine.[12] The market enables the owner to minimize the social opportunity cost of exploiting his resource simply by minimizing his total costs. Bid and asked prices of resources provide owners with information as well as the incentives to use that information for allocating resources efficiently,

11. See John Hanner, "Government Response to the Buffalo Hide Trade – 1871–1883," *Journal of Law and Economics* 24 (October 1981): 239–71.
12. For a more thorough treatment of markets in a resource setting, see Richard Stroup and John Baden, "Externality, Property Rights, and the Management of Our National Forests," *The Journal of Law and Economics* 16 (1973): 303–12.

thereby serving others. Similarly, consumers are informed by prices of the value *others* place on a given resource. In an open market, no one consumes or controls a good desired more by others, as measured by the size of the others' bids.

The benefits of diversity, individual freedom, adaptiveness to changing conditions, the production of information, and even a certain equity derive from this market system. Diversity flourishes because there is no single, centralized decision maker. Instead, many asset owners and entrepreneurs, making their own individual decisions, compete over resource allocations. Those who correctly anticipate people's desires are rewarded the most. Those who envisioned a retail market for television in the 1930s and 1940s and acted on their vision, for example, may have been amply rewarded in the 1950s.

This system preserves individual freedom since those who support and wish to participate in each activity may do so on the basis of willing consent. If I want more logs for my log house, my neighbor need not be concerned. I must pay at least as much for the logs as anyone else would, and in so doing I give up purchasing power that could be used to buy other items. No shortage will result. Adaptiveness is encouraged in both management and consumer activities, since prices provide immediate information and incentives for action as soon as changes are seen. In the political arena any change in resource policy requires convincing a majority of the voters, or the bureaucracy, of the benefits such change would generate. The market system, however, permits individuals who envision scarcities or opportunities in the future to buy or sell resources and develop expertise that may redirect resource use. If their expectations about the future prove correct, they will profit. Losses from foolish diversions of resources, on the other hand, ultimately channel those resources away from inefficient or little valued ventures. From this marvelous adaptive quality, we get both television and Edsels. Successes quickly draw imitators. Losers are quickly dropped, and unsuccessful planners are disciplined by losses.

Information, produced as a byproduct of bids offered and prices asked, is vital to the coordination of individual plans.[13] The market

13. Economists of the Austrian school emphasize the role of the entrepreneur who, in his search for profit, finds higher valued uses for resources. See, for example, Ludwig von Mises, *Human Action* (New Haven, Conn.: Yale University Press, 1949); and Israel Kirzner, *Competition and Entrepreneurship* (Chicago: University of Chicago Press, 1973).

pricing system provides a tangible measure of how individuals evaluate a particular product or service relative to others that use the same resources. Without a market system of exchange such assessments are virtually impossible to make, thereby rendering rational management of nonmarketed activities difficult if not impossible. No manager can make productive resource allocation decisions without knowing input and output values, without knowing, for example, how much people are willing to sacrifice for a thousand board feet of lumber. When rights are privately held and transferable, prices yield the necessary information about the relative value of alternative resource uses—information that is concise, measurable, comparable, and largely devoid of distortion.

A management system based on private property rights also provides a certain equity by having those people who use a resource or who wish to reserve it pay for it by sacrificing some of their wealth. Where natural resources are publicly owned but used by only a few, the sale of those resources could provide a new measure of equity. The proceeds from the sale of assets now in the public domain could be distributed widely in cash or in lower taxes. Alternatively, they could be invested to reduce the national debt or used to cope with the actuarial deficit of the social security system (see chapter 9 for more on this suggestion). In a market, those who use the resources would receive from sale proceeds their share of the wealth and would then be required to pay for resources they use, whether for recreation, timber harvest, or research.

PRIVATE AND TRANSFERABLE
PROPERTY RIGHTS

Markets can generate both equity and efficiency. Their very essence requires decentralized decision making that can promote flexibility and individual freedom, as well as the information from which rational management of resources is made possible. Yet these advantages will materialize only when property rights to each resource are privately held and easily transferable, ensuring that decision makers will have an incentive to identify the highest value of their resources, including their value to others. In the absence of such clearly defined and enforceable rights, resources may be utilized by individuals who need not compensate or outbid anyone for their use, resulting in substantial waste.

Private ownership of property rights alone is insufficient to secure efficient resource use. If rights are not easily transferable, owners may, for example, have little incentive to conserve resources for which others might be willing to pay if transfer were possible. Transferability ensures that a resource owner must reject all bids for the resource in order to continue ownership and use. Thus, if ownership is retained, the cost to others is made real and explicit.

Private and transferable property rights mandate consideration of alternative users' interests. Any failure to do so imposes economic penalties on the owner. On the other hand, nonprivate or nontransferable property rights often result in inefficiency and waste, as well as a potential indifference to others' interests. When rights are private and transferable, a decentralized market provides diversity, individual freedom, flexibility, information, and equity, since the interests of nonowners are unavoidably observed and respected.[14]

MARKET FAILURE AND POTENTIAL REMEDIES

It is important to acknowledge and describe market failures, their root causes, and their potential remedies in order to proceed to compare market with nonmarket outcomes. Market failure occurs when property rights are inadequately specified or are not controlled by those who can benefit personally by putting the resources to their most highly valued uses. Though both champions and critics of markets have long recognized the potential pitfalls of monopoly, externalities, public goods and common pool problems, transaction costs, and inequities, seldom are they traced to their origins.[15] Yet remedies cannot be developed, nor can the role of government management be properly assessed, without first understanding the causes of market failure.

Many have argued that unfettered market operations would produce monopolies in which single individuals or firms controlling the

14. The workings of the market are explained from a property rights approach, with a minimum of jargon, in Armen Alchian and William Allen, *University Economics*, 3d ed. (Belmont, Calif.: Wadsworth, 1972); James Gwartney and Richard Stroup, *Economics: Private and Public Choice*, 2d ed. (New York: Academic Press, 1980); Paul Heyne, *The Economic Way of Thinking*, 3d ed. (Chicago: SRA, 1980); and Svetozar Pejovich, *Fundamentals of Economics: A Property Rights Approach* (Dallas: The Fisher Institute, 1979).

15. For a systematic treatment of the "accepted wisdom" on market failure, see Francis M. Bator, "The Anatomy of Market Failure," *The Quarterly Journal of Economics* (August 1958), pp. 351-79.

entire supply of a resource would limit output in order to increase price. In the absence of any satisfactory substitutes, the resource owner would benefit from these restrictions on production. Under these circumstances, production of additional units could be sustained at prices lower than those set by the monopoly, yet sufficiently high that other investors, were they able to gain access to the resource in question, would be willing to develop it. In this case, monopoly would result in pronounced inefficiency.[16]

A second market failure, that of externalities, is especially prominent in discussions lamenting the market misallocation of natural resources. Externalities refer to the separation of responsibility from authority in resource decision making. In other words, an externality exists when some results of a decision do not affect the decision maker.

Both negative and positive externalities can develop. Perhaps the most often condemned negative externality is air pollution. Why should some individuals, for example, suffer harm from smoke produced by others? Such pollution is often both inequitable as well as inefficient in the event that the costs of reducing the pollution are actually less than the damages such a reduction would eliminate. But as long as the decision maker is shielded from the costs or damages of his actions, negative externalities will abound.

Positive externalities present a symmetrical problem, appearing when a decision maker's actions yield benefits that cannot be captured by the decision maker.[17] If my neighbor continues to grow wheat or raise livestock on his land rather than strip-mine the coal below, I enjoy the view without having to pay him. Therefore, of course, he need not consider my values when negotiating with coal buyers and deciding how to use his land. In general, activities leading to positive externalities tend to be underproduced.

Both negative and positive externalities result from imperfectly defined property rights. If runoff from a farmer's land pollutes a stream, a negative externality occurs simply because the stream is not owned by anyone. If rights to the stream were privately held, a polluter would be liable for pollution damages in the same way he

16. Nearly all introductory economics texts cover the general problem of monopoly, including the four cited in note 14.

17. The following discussion of positive externalities is drawn from Richard Stroup and John Baden, "Property Rights and Natural Resource Management," *Literature of Liberty* 2 (September–December 1979): 11.

would be liable for damaging his neighbor's house.[18] The courts would enforce existing rights if damage could be proven. A resource whose rights are unassigned is likely to be abused.[19]

Positive externalities, such as the inability to charge a neighbor for the aesthetic pleasure provided by one's apple orchard, for example, also represent an absence of the right to control and exclude others from the enjoyment of all output from the land resource. Since no compensation for providing the view is received, the aesthetic values of others play no part in the owner's decision to retain or bulldoze the orchard and put it to other uses.[20]

The Logic of the Commons

The presence of so-called public goods and common pool resources, in which every management decision has external effects on others, presents another set of market problems. Public goods are those goods that, once produced, are available for anyone to use, whether or not they have contributed to their production.[21] Individuals thus may become "free riders," benefiting from goods that others have provided. Because the benefits associated with public goods are not necessarily paid for by all who enjoy them, market behavior generally underproduces such goods.

Particularly problematic regarding natural resources is the common pool problem. "A common pool is like a soda being drawn

18. See *Corpus Juris Secundum*, vol. 66, p. 9461. This common law approach is being supplemented by statutory laws that proclaim the mere existence of a pollution source a nuisance, apart from demonstrated damage. Such laws are currently being challenged in the courts.

19. Note that if property rights to clean air were easily enforced, pollution would still be produced, but only in efficient amounts. Polluters would compensate those damaged and would reduce pollution until further reductions were more costly than if they fully compensated all those harmed. A different approach considers negative externalities as a failure of law regarding liability. The implications of alternative liability laws are examined in Roland McKean, "Products Liability: Implications of Some Changing Property Rights," *Quarterly Journal of Economics* 84 (November 1970): 611-26.

20. See Ronald Coase, "The Problem of Social Cost," *The Journal of Law and Economics* 4 (October 1960): 1-44. Coase shows that in the absence of transaction costs it does not matter *who* owns the resource, only that wealth will change.

21. In his original definition of a *public good*, Paul Samuelson stated that one individual's consumption of a public good led to no reduction in others' consumption. See Paul Samuelson, "The Pure Theory of Public Expenditures," *Review of Economics and Statistics* 36 (1954): 347-53.

down by several small boys, each with a straw. The 'rule of capture' is in effect. The contents of the container belong to no one boy until he 'captures' it through his straw."[22] The relevance of this problem to current institutions that define ownership of oil (or in some cases underground water) is evident. Ownership of these resources is recognized only when someone actually extracts the resource from the ground, thus providing an incentive for different individuals each tapping the same reservoir to withdraw the resource as quickly as possible. This behavior may misallocate the oil or water over time. Furthermore, because of geological factors, such practices may even reduce the total volume that can be extracted from the well.[23]

Markets need not inevitably present public goods and common pool problems. Rather, it is the incomplete nature of existing property rights arrangements that has given rise to these problems. If those who failed to pay could be excluded from the benefits of current so-called public goods, no problem would exist. Demands for the goods would be reflected in offers made to purchase them. The same is true for resources subject to common pool problems. Establishing property rights to resources currently beset by overuse or underproduction because of public goods and common pool considerations would virtually eliminate these problems.

Transaction costs pose another problem for efficient market operations. Under ideal market conditions, no transaction costs would arise.[24] All individuals affected by a particular transaction would be included in the decision-making process. If there were no costs associated with defining and enforcing property rights, nor any costs of identifying and undertaking mutually beneficial exchange, all exchanges in which benefits outweighed costs would be undertaken. However, ideally efficient markets do not prevail, and some transac-

22. This discussion of the common pool problem derives largely from Richard Stroup and John Baden, "Property Rights and Natural Resource Management." The quote is from p. 12.

23. If many well-owners pump more rapidly from many pools, ignoring the "user cost" or reduced availability from each pool later, then oil market prices can be depressed. When this happened in the United States in the 1930s, the government gained control of oil well production. See Edward Mitchell, U.S. Energy Policy: A Primer (Washington, D.C.: American Enterprise Institute, 1974). For a general treatment of problems associated with common pool resources, see Garrett Hardin and John Baden, eds., Managing the Commons (San Francisco: W.H. Freeman and Company, 1977), especially Hardin's "The Tragedy of the Commons," pp. 16–30.

24. For further discussions on transaction costs (the cost of reaching a final bargain among parties), see Furubotn and Pejovich, "Property Rights and Economic Theory"; and Cheung, "The Structure of a Contract."

tion costs do, in fact, almost always enter into market calculations. Thus, alternatives that might overcome the transaction costs associated with voluntary market exchange merit theoretical consideration.

Thus far, each of the problems discussed—monopoly, externalities, public goods, common pools, and transaction costs—has referred to failures in market efficiency. Though efficiency is certainly a significant indication of market success, the more subjective goal of equity must also be addressed. If efficiency means making the largest pie from our given resources, equity is the determination of how that pie is divided among the population. But which division of the economic pie is most equitable? Some may equate equity with equality, arguing that a more equal distribution of income is more equitable, or that equity requires a more equal distribution of the means of production. Even for those who do not equate equality with equity, how the pie is sliced will still be of primary importance.[25] The private property paradigm emphasizes that individuals tend to seek control over the largest possible piece of pie. Thus, how that pie is initially distributed and what rules govern the distribution have significant implications for the overall equity of the system.

If the market system fails to distribute costs and benefits in ways that are perceived as equitable, individuals may seek alternative methods of influencing that distribution. Efforts emerge to redistribute benefits to low income citizens, or pleas are voiced to curb what are considered windfall profits from crude oil. Both are symptomatic of general concerns about the equity of markets.

Whether in pursuit of greater equity or efficiency, many persons have increasingly turned to governmental institutions to achieve preferred allocation of natural resources. This search for government solutions persists despite the government's tarnished performance as a natural resource manager.

PUBLIC, NONTRANSFERABLE RIGHTS IN A GOVERNMENTAL SETTING

An activist government has been lauded as the last line of defense between the bulldozer and the bald eagle. A corollary to this belief con-

---

25. The growing importance of equity is discussed in Fred Hirsch, *Social Limits to Growth* (Cambridge: Harvard University Press, 1976); Robert A. Nisbet, *Twilight of Authority* (New York: Oxford University Press, 1975); and Daniel Bell, *Cultural Contradictions of Capitalism* (New York: Basic Books, 1976).

tends that those involved with governmental regulation are motivated by incentives that are incorrectly analyzed by economists, whose theories apply only to a perfectly competitive market. It is thought that even though economic analysis and economic principles can explain behavior in markets, they have little bearing on governmental actions, since motives change when people enter government service. Yet these contentions are incorrect. Economic principles apply in all settings, including bureaucracies and among primitive tribes (see especially chapters 3 and 4).

Though current market systems allocate resources imperfectly, even many critics of markets agree that governmental efforts to correct market imperfections have ensured neither efficiency nor equity.[26] Furthermore, there is a growing awareness that self-interest is not absent in the public sector and that economic analysis is applicable and even necessary if the actions and goals of the public sector are to be understood.

The pioneering contributions of Anthony Downs, James Buchanan and Gordon Tullock, Mancur Olson, and William Niskanen have led to a developing awareness of the problems of representative government.[27] Their analyses show some promise of approaching the rigor and predictive capacity of the economic theory of the firm.[28] While precise predictions regarding public sector decision making may not be possible, some general statements may be made with confidence.

26. Economists are still struggling with the theory of regulations, but not fruitlessly. For a technical approach see, for example, George Stigler, "The Theory of Economic Regulation," *Bell Journal of Economics and Management Science* 2 (1971): 3–21; and Sam Peltzman, "Toward a More General Theory of Regulation," *The Journal of Law and Economics* 11 (1976): 211-40. The problems of governmental (bureaucratic) control of resources are analyzed in William A. Niskanen, Jr., *Bureaucracy and Representative Government* (Chicago: Aldine-Atherton, 1971); and Thomas Borcherding, ed., *Budgets and Bureaucrats* (Durham, N.C.: Duke University Press, 1977). These problems are discussed in a natural resource context in John Baden and Richard Stroup, "The Environmental Costs of Government Action," *Policy Review* 4 (1978): 23-26.

27. Anthony Downs, *An Economic Theory of Democracy* (New York: Harper, 1957); James Buchanan and Gordon Tullock, *The Calculus of Consent* (Ann Arbor: University of Michigan Press, 1962); Mancur Olson, Jr., *The Logic of Collective Action* (New York: Schocken Books, 1965); and Niskanen, *Bureaucracy and Representative Government.*

28. For a relatively nontechnical presentation of the economics of government failure, see Gwartney and Stroup, *Economics: Private and Public Choice,* chap. 32. See also Richard B. McKenzie and Gordon Tullock, *Modern Political Economy: An Introduction to Political Economy* (New York: McGraw Hill, 1978), chaps. 5 and 6; and William Mitchell, *The Anatomy of Government Failure* (Los Angeles: International Institute for Economic Research, 1979).

Using the property rights approach in which decision makers act to advance their own perceived interests, we observe that, as in market systems with imperfect property rights and transaction costs, public-sector decision makers are not held fully accountable for their actions.

The public sector provides no incentives for politicians and bureaucrats to resist pressures from special interests or to manage natural resources efficiently. On the contrary, such resistance may even hinder the public decision maker's career. Presumably, those turning to government to resolve natural resource problems earnestly seek more efficient and equitable management. Why, then, are public officials not held more accountable for managing resources accordingly?

Five factors tend to undermine that accountability. First, no citizen has either the time or the resources to analyze every policy issue. Nor is every citizen able personally to influence decisions regarding most complex public policy issues. Given these constraints, the intelligent citizen's ignorance about most public policy matters is understandable.

Second, although no individuals attempt to analyze or influence *all* government policies, some do attempt to influence specific policies in which they have a pronounced interest. The result is a medley of narrowly focused, highly self-interested groups that wield tremendous influence, each over its particular policy domain. These special interest groups are able to dominate a particular policy domain precisely because others with more diffuse interests regarding such policies have little incentive to articulate their views.[29]

The system of political representation further limits the accountability of policymakers. Voters themselves have no direct input on individual issues. They merely elect representatives who, in turn, make the decisions regarding all policy issues. Such a system obviously records individual preferences imperfectly, if at all.[30]

A congressman or senator votes on hundreds of issues each year. The message sent (the vote cast) by even a thoroughly informed, decisive voter is garbled. While the voter agrees with his favorite candidate on some important issues, there may be serious disagreement

29. For more rigor and detail on this and related aspects of the political process, see Gordon Tullock, *Toward a Mathematics of Politics* (Ann Arbor: University of Michigan Press, 1967).

30. On this point, see Gordon Tullock, *Private Wants and Public Means* (New York: Basic Books, 1970), pp. 107-14.

on many other issues that are judged less important by that voter. By contrast, in the private sector the citizen can "vote for" tires made by one company and toasters made by another. His choices in a market are precisely recorded.

A fourth factor further weakens the incentive for efficient natural resource management. Many resource issues have significant long-term implications for future generations. How and which resources are developed today will affect future generations. Yet precisely what those future costs and benefits might be are generally poorly understood, especially by the average citizen, who remains ill-informed about such issues. Thus, most individuals evaluate the performance of politicians and bureaucrats not according to how well they shepherd resources for the future, but according to whether or not their decisions have produced current *net* benefits.

A government decision maker can seldom gain political support by locking resources away from voters to benefit the unborn. Charitable instincts toward future resource users are unaided by (and are, in fact, countered by) self-interest if the resources are publicly owned. Charity toward others at the expense of voting constituents does not usually contribute to political survival. So we can expect governmental policy to be shortsighted, especially in comparison to the long time-frames necessary for carrying out many natural resource policies. Future benefits are more difficult to measure and future costs are easy to ignore. In addition, there is no "voice of the future" in government equivalent to the rising market price of an increasingly valuable resource. The wise public resource manager who forgoes current benefits cannot personally profit from doing so.

Yet another widespread—and incorrect—assumption is that governmental intervention in private markets can be expected to produce farsighted decisions, whereas actions taken to enlarge profits or individual wealth are normally shortsighted. This belief springs from the conviction that future generations have a property right in current resources; that is, there are transgenerational property rights for the unborn. The major implication of this and similar thinking is that a market mechanism, unlike collective control, deprives future generations of resources. This belief arises in turn from the conviction that resources are being rapidly depleted, although prices for many natural minerals are in fact declining. This obvious inconsistency aside, let us assume that future generations are in some fashion granted a property right in this generation's available resources. Can the government protect the interests of these future generations better than the market?

Enter the speculator. Even though "speculator" is a term often used derisively, it merely describes a market participant who performs a service consistent with the desires of his harshest critics: He defers consumption and thereby saves for the future by paying a market price higher than any other bidder who seeks resources for present use. Indeed, exploitation will occur only when all speculative bids have been overcome.

In effect, farsighted outcomes are made possible through the activities of speculators who have an incentive to protect resources for future sale and use because such preservation may benefit them. For example, the owner of an Indiana woodlot may think that his old-growth white oak trees should be saved rather than harvested. Any concern he has for the future is powerfully influenced by how much he can gain by hoarding his resource, which is becoming more scarce and valuable, and selling it later to other hoarders or speculators. The speculator thus acts as a middleman between the present and the future.[31] His position is similar to that of another middleman, a broker of Florida oranges. By purchasing the oranges and shipping them to Montana, the fruit broker acts *as if* he cares about the desires of Montanans. He bids oranges away from Florida buyers in order to send them to Montana. The woodlot owner may act in the same way, taking wood off the market and "transporting" it into the future by failing to cut it. Since the property rights are transferable, the speculator can do well for himself while he does good for future resource users. He can profit from the transaction if he has guessed correctly. This incentive to look to the future contrasts sharply with the incentives faced in the public sector.

Private ownership allows the owner to capture the full capital value of his resource, and thus economic incentive directs him to maintain its long-term capital value. The owner of the resource, be it a fishery, a mine, or a forest, wants to produce today, tomorrow, and ten years from now; and with a renewable resource he will attempt to maintain a sustained yield. Do farmers consume their seed corn or slaughter the last of their prime breeding cattle even when prices are especially high? In contrast, when a resource is owned by everyone,

---

31. This discussion of speculation generally follows a similar discussion in Stroup and Baden, "Property Rights and Natural Resource Management," p. 17.

the only way in which individuals can capture its economic value is to exploit the resource before someone else does.

A final factor dictates against efficient resource management within the public sector: There is no tangible internal measure of efficiency. Private sector firms whose use of resources (as measured by cost) exceeds the value of what they produce (as measured by revenue) lose money and go out of business. Their failure benefits society by removing control of scarce resources from those who use them inefficiently. Eliminating this mechanism from the market system is probably the most significant cost of government bailouts of private firms.

Government decision makers operate without this internal check on efficiency. The funding for government bureaus derives not from profits resulting from efficient use of resources, but from federal treasury "bailouts" and budget allocations. Public sector decision makers operate with no concrete measure of efficiency because their survival does not depend on the difference between costs and benefits. Indeed, the incentive is to expand rather than to economize.[32] An expanding bureau allows its administrators more opportunities for advancement and achievement, greater scope for power, and less need for unpleasant budget trimming and layoff decisions.

A REALISTIC ANALYSIS?

Our analysis has resolutely criticized decision making in the public sector. Such criticism is not overly cynical. Rather, our assessment simply recognizes that individuals, not organizations or societies, make decisions and that individuals tend to act according to their own perceived interests.

Charitable instincts are important, but the forces of simple self-interest are relentless. In order to be useful and beneficial to society as a whole, an institution must relate authority—that is, command

32. The public choice literature, taking a property rights approach, is developing an increasingly sophisticated set of models to explain bureaucratic behavior. See, for example, Jean-Luc Mique and Gerard Belanger, "Toward a General Theory of Managerial Discretion," *Public Choice* 17 (1974); Niskanen, *Bureaucracy and Representative Government*; Gordon Tullock, *The Politics of Bureaucracy* (Washington, D.C.: Public Affairs Press, 1965); and Oliver Williamson, *The Economics of Discretionary Behavior: Managerial Objectives in a Theory of the Firm* (Englewood Cliffs, N.J.: Prentice-Hall, 1964).

over resources—to personal responsibility for the costs and benefits that flow from decisions.

The market relies on private property rights to hold individuals responsible for their actions. Imperfectly defined, enforced, or transferable rights generate market failures. Government is different. Representative democracy depends on informed voters and their elected representatives to ensure the accountability of governmental decision makers. Yet existing institutions and incentives provide neither informed voters nor accountability. A general understanding of the model presented above—an understanding shared by the authors of the *Federalist Papers*—can foster reforms that are likely to improve social welfare.

Chapter 3

THE NATIVE AMERICAN AS
A RESOURCE MANAGER

Earth Day in April 1970 ushered in a decade of optimism among environmentalists who assumed that good resource policy would ensue automatically from a combination of good intentions and competent bureaucrats. This assumption is not only unrealistic, but derives from two naive political assumptions whose implications are socially expensive.

The first assumption is that problems in resource management can be solved by appointing and electing the right people to make decisions and set policy. The second is that culture can "rewire" people so that the public interest becomes self-interest. Ordinary self-interest can then be eliminated.

The first assumption takes it for granted that resolving fundamental problems depends not on providing appropriate incentives, but on appointing or electing the "right" individuals to make decisions. According to this view, individuals with the "right" values have different goals than those with the wrong values. This belief relies on the questionable notion that those who make so many "incorrect" decisions in the marketplace will manage to make "correct" ballot box decisions and elect the "right" people. Why this should be expected is, of course, unexplained. The second assumption contends that people can consistently put aside their own interests and act only for the so-called public good. Although both of these assumptions may appeal to some people's nobler instincts, their policy implications may be expensive to sustain.

There is, however, an alternative approach to attaining social goals through voluntary cooperation among self-interested individuals. This alternative is based on some basic principles of human behavior:[1]

(1) People choose purposefully, tending to pick the options from which they expect to benefit the most.

(2) People respond to relative costs and prices. If an action is made more costly, it will be taken less frequently; if it is rewarded more, it will be taken more frequently. In short, incentives matter.

(3) Information is scarce and costly. As a result, ignorance is often rational, especially when the outcome will not be controlled by the individual's decision. The rewards for learning and information gathering are small, for example, for the person whose vote is seldom decisive.

(4) An economic system, like an ecological system, is strongly interconnected. A policy may have its intended effects, but it will probably produce unintended side effects as well.

(5) There is no free lunch when the system is operating efficiently. Collective decision making and the governmental provision of goods can break the link between an individual's consumption and his payment, but then others must pay.

(6) Exchange is not a zero sum game. Even without added production, everyone can be made better off when goods and services are moved to higher valued uses. Higher profits, for example, can be accompanied by increased consumer well-being.

These principles are empirical, subject to refutation.[2] By examining cross-cultural data it is possible, at least tentatively, to confirm them. In particular, we shall illustrate through such data the validity of the first and second principles.

1. This description of human behavior is taken from "Good Intentions and Self-Interest: Lessons from the American Indian," in *Earth Day Reconsidered*, ed. John Baden (Washington, D.C.: The Heritage Foundation, 1980), p. 5. See also, John Baden, Richard Stroup, and Wally Thurman, "Myths, Admonitions and Rationality: The American Indian as a Resource Manager," *Economic Inquiry* 19 (January 1981): 132–43.

2. See, for example, Heyne, *The Economic Way of Thinking*; and Gwartney and Stroup, *Economics: Private and Public Choice*.

Are there cultures in which self-interest is subservient to ecological harmony? If so, are such societies lead by the "right" people, properly motivated by nonmarket incentives, or have entire cultures been "rewired" and converted? Have they been able to internalize the public interest as their own?

Social scientists disagree on whether cultural norms determine behavior or vice versa. The question is complex and not very amenable to scientific resolution. However, there is one case in which the controversy has been played out in detail—the relationship between primitive people's attitudes and beliefs and their behavior toward the natural environment.

As political economists, we shall ignore the strict question of causality. By applying microeconomics in its predictive sense to this relationship we shall ask whether economic theory can successfully predict primitive people's environmental behavior from observable phenomena. Going one step further, can we successfully predict how these cultures addressed the same environmental issues and resource management questions with which we wrestle? An affirmative answer would support our inclination to discard or at least downgrade serious consideration of the economic fallacies under discussion and move toward solutions based on incentives.

NATIVE AMERICANS AND THE ENVIRONMENT

Native North American cultures varied immensely, with tribes ranging from the simplest hunting-gathering bands to empires, from the extreme poverty of the Great Basin to the relative affluence of the northwest coast. Nonetheless, many believe that these highly diverse groups shared a common reverence for the land and the interdependencies of nature. The implications of this view are perhaps most explicitly expressed by Vine Deloria, who wrote that the white man "must quickly adopt not just the contemporary Indian world view but the ancient Indian world view to survive."[3]

Native Americans are believed to have been totally nonmaterialistic, limiting consumption to what was actually needed rather than consuming to impress another lodge or family. Rather than being influenced by price, measures of present value, or the decisions of

3. Vine Deloria, *We Talk, You Listen* (New York: Macmillan, 1970), p. 195.

bureaucratic managers, it is argued that cultural traditions that incorporated generations of ecological understanding guided their actions.

Throughout North America, there was a high incidence of nature being incorporated into native religions. The material offered by Vilhjalmur Stefansson on the Eskimo, Robert Lowie on the Crow, and Edward Spicer on the Southwest tribes strongly supports this statement.[4] This same reverence for nature extended to the use of natural resources, reflected, for example, in the Blackfoot discovery of over one hundred different uses for the buffalo.

It appears, then, that the Indian culture embodied most of the requirements of spaceship earth. But to agree with Deloria that the adoption of Indian values is a requisite to man's successful accommodation to the environment leaves one with little policy leverage. How are the necessary changes in values to be fostered? Similarly, to rely on value shifts to explain behavioral changes produces a model of little predictive power. Is it possible, instead, to explain environmental behavior without appealing to differences or changes in environmental values? Economic theory indicates that it is.

Economists maintain that all people respond to relative prices—that is, to real opportunity costs. The law of demand, simply stated, asserts that the more a person must relinquish to obtain a good, the less that good will be demanded. In addition, the principle of diminishing marginal utility states that the more of a good a person has, the less he will give up for an additional unit. Thus we would expect that today's American may be willing to sacrifice to protect highly valued endangered species, but we cannot expect him to make a similar sacrifice for a commonplace wild animal.

If these laws are correct and widely applicable, culture will not negate them. Indian cultures should be consistent with these laws, valuing environmental goods (natural resources) as do other cultures. When the cost to users of these goods is high, little will be demanded; when the cost is low, more will be demanded.

---

4. See Vilhjalmur Stefansson, *My Life with the Eskimo* (New York: Macmillan, 1913); Robert Lowie, *The Crow Indians* (New York: Rinehart, 1935); and Edward H. Spicer, *Cycles of Conquest: The Impact of Spain, Mexico, and the United States on the Indians of the Southwest, 1533–1960* (Tucson: University of Arizona Press, 1962).

THE PLAINS INDIANS AND THE
FUGITIVE BUFFALO

The Indians of the American Plains are among the most well known and eulogized of all tribal peoples. Prior to the introduction of the horse, the capture of a buffalo was comparatively rare, making it a scarce, highly valued and, therefore, fully used resource. The legendary resourcefulness of these Indians is rooted in their remarkably efficient use of the buffalo, including horns, long hair, short hair, tail, tail skin, tail tassel, eye sockets, and ribs.

Summer skins from the bulls were often left untanned after the hair had been removed. When the skins dried, they became the hard, tough rawhide of a dozen uses, such as moccasin soles, belts, all sorts of lashings, and indestructible, waterproof containers for supplies.

Buffalo horns were shaped into spoons, cups, and ladles. The long shaggy hair from the head was braided into rope. The short soft hair was used for stuffing game balls. The tail with the tuft of hair left on the end became a fly whisk, or the skin from the tail could be made into a knife sheath with the hair tassel for a decoration.

Buffalo bones were used for making long awls and hide scrapers. . . . Rib bones made sled runners, pieces of bone were shaped into small counters for gambling games—and these uses do not exhaust this list by any means.[5]

To say that the Plains Indians did not waste the buffalo is to say that they made efficient use of a scarce resource. This does not in any way indicate, however, that all resources were so frugally conserved. In fact, we might find that relatively plentiful resources were liberally expended, perhaps even wasted, in order to harvest the highly valued buffalo.

The introduction of the horse, steel tools, firearms, and other technological adaptations in effect lowered the price of the buffalo. As the price fell, patterns of use changed as well, and many buffalo were killed during this period merely for the tongue and two strips of back strap. Ultimately, these practices resulted in the buffalo's disappearance from some of its original habitat. As Earl F. Murphy states, "Only the simplicity of weaponry and the small numbers of these nomadic peoples kept the buffalo from meeting its fate two centuries sooner."[6]

5. Francis Haines, *The Buffalo* (New York: Thomas Y. Crowell, 1970), p. 27.
6. Earl F. Murphy, *Governing Nature* (New York: Quadrangle Press, 1967), p. 99.

This shift in technology was augmented by the Plains Indian's newly acquired access to the white man's market for hides. Thus there were two sources of increased demand for buffalo on the hoof. One resulted from the lower "costs" of harvest and the other was a new use of buffalo, sales. Both generated greater rates of buffalo kills.

The Plains Indian behavior reveals an *efficient* behavioral adjustment by individual tribes to changing prices but a socially *inefficient* management of a common property resource. The fugitive nature of the resource, coupled with the number of tribes utilizing it, resulted in high transaction costs that made delineation of property rights and management of the buffalo as a renewable resource impossible. Even though Indian cultures held an ideological reverence for nature, it was not always a sufficient force to guide behavior.

The experience of the Plains Indians suggests that without clearly defined and enforced property rights efficient resource use is unlikely regardless of the user's ideology. Communally owned resources actually promote ecologically damaging behavior. For the Plains Indians, therefore, the individual benefited from hunting additional buffalo, while the costs of depleting the herd were distributed among all potential hunters. Again, understanding the negative externalities inherent in the utilization of such common pool resources helps predict the buffalo harvest as the hunters' economic circumstances changed. In such a context, the hunter does not bear the full costs of the hunt. Others bear most of the cost of the extra kills, and overuse can be anticipated.

As with any market failure, when property rights are poorly defined—in this case because of a fugitive resource, high transaction costs, and a common pool resource—the party with the authority to act (the hunter) is isolated from the consequences of his action (depletive exploitation). Authority is separated from responsibility, and the social cost exceeds the private gain.

There are examples of successful resource management in the face of common pool problems and negative externalities. If, as our analysis has indicated, behavior can be explained as rational responses to relative prices, it is important to find out what mechanisms confront individuals with the "right" set of prices. What cultural institutions and incentives determine the costs and benefits perceived by individuals?

PROPERTY RIGHTS INNOVATIONS
AND THE COASTAL FUR TRADE

Prior to Frank Speck's article in 1915 on the private hunting territories of the Montagnais Indians on the Labrador Peninsula, the institution of private property was commonly considered to be a late stage in cultural development, incompatible with primitive society. Indeed, among native North Americans, common ownership of hunting grounds was almost universal. Speck and others spent years studying the Montagnais; the following paragraphs briefly summarize their work.

The Montagnais Indians were primarily hunters who subsisted on large game such as caribou and small fur-bearers such as beaver.[7] Before trade with Europeans developed, there was little pressure on these resources. Harvest rates were below carrying capacity, and the tribes hunted communally, sharing in the harvest. But when French fur trade routes were established in the early 1600s, an incentive to overexploit the resource emerged.

As the beaver increased in value and scarcity, it could be predicted that the common ownership of hunting grounds would lead to depletion and localized extinction. Counter to the conventional wisdom that denies such a culturally advanced institution in primitive societies, the beaver, in contrast to the buffalo, were protected by the evolution of private property rights among their hunters.

By the early to mid-eighteenth century, the establishment of private hunting grounds was almost complete, and the Montagnais were managing the beaver on a sustained yield basis. Eleanor Leacock notes that trappers readily adopted conservation practices when they were able to personally collect the benefits.[8] "The Western Montagnais farms his territory by marking his houses, ascertaining the number of beavers in them, and always leaving at least a pair."[9] This system of private ownership developed parallel to the fur trade. As

7. Probably the first to subject the Montagnais to economic analysis was Harold Demsetz in "Toward a Theory of Property Rights," *American Economic Review* 57 (May 1967): 347–73. See also Frank G. Speck, "Land Ownership Among Hunting Peoples in Primitive America and the World's Marginal Areas," *Twenty-second International Congress of Americanists* 2 (1926).

8. Eleanor Leacock, "The Montagnais 'Hunting Territory' and the Fur Trade," *American Anthropologist* 56 (1954): 5.

9. Ibid., p. 35.

Leacock noted, there was "an unmistakable correlation between early centers of trade and the oldest and most complete development of the hunting territory."[10] Predictably, the system was the most extensive where the incentives were the greatest.

Why did this successful property rights institution crumble under heavy French fur trapping competition? Remember that a viable property right includes the right to exclude others and the ability to enforce that exclusion. Though the Montagnais had developed private property rights, they were unable to enforce them against the intrusion of the white trapper in the nineteenth century. Because the Indians could not exclude the white trappers from the benefits of conservation, both raced to trap out the beaver.

In spite of this unhappy ending, the primitive Montagnais culture showed that it was capable of designing institutions that promoted the efficient use of resources through an appropriate incentive structure. Additional examples of the successful management of common pool resources are numerous among primitive peoples.[11] But whether such success occurred seems to hinge on how easily the institutional devices could be applied. That is, resources were conserved if the returns from management were greater than the administrative and enforcement costs, usually in areas where the resource was geographically concentrated and appropriation was limited.

The success of the beaver trappers relative to the buffalo hunters may be traced simply to their different institutional structures. In turn, the institutional differences can be explained by the fundamentally different characteristics of the resources. Buffalo are a fugitive resource. Beaver, on the other hand, are sedentary and thus amenable to private appropriations. Nor were the transaction costs among a relatively homogeneous group of tribes such as the Montagnais as high as those among the warring Plains tribes, making institutional accommodation easier to achieve.

It seems clear that the "right" Indians with different incentives and the "rewired" Indians seem to have been reserved for twentieth century sociologists, anthropologists, and fiction writers to discover. Consideration of the Indian experience, however, strongly supports our claim that the beliefs (1) that resource management can be

10. Ibid., p. 12.
11. See R. F. Heizer, "Primitive Man as an Ecologic Factor," *Kroeber Anthropological Society Papers*, no. 15 (Berkeley and Los Angeles: University of California Press, 1955); and Speck, "Land Ownership," p. 323.

solved by getting the right people to make decisions, and (2) that culture can "rewire" people so that public interest becomes self-interest hold little, if any, truth.

CULTURE AND ENVIRONMENTAL QUALITY

The claim that an environmentally sensitive culture promotes environmentally sensitive behavior is inconsistent with data from native North American cultures. Can we conclude, then, that culture has nothing to do with the way man treats his natural environment? Is the "land ethic" advocated by Aldo Leopold to be dismissed as unimportant? [12] Not at all. Clearly, there is a relationship between beliefs, values, and man's treatment of his environment. That relationship is not as simple, however, as saying that an environmentally sensitive culture leads to environmentally sensitive behavior.

Most environmental problems faced by any society result from property being held in common. The potential for solving a common pool problem largely depends on the physical details of the particular resource. But unless society's institutions protect the commons, as the Montagnais protected their beaver stocks, those who *fail* to practice conservation will be rewarded. The perverse results of such incentives are obvious.

Certainly, if the culture changes so that people respect, understand, and value environmental systems more, greater pressure will be placed on policymakers to protect our common pool resources. This pressure can lead to legal and institutional modifications that produce a different pattern of information and incentives. Since it appears that people do respond as predicted by economic theory, these institutions and laws can encourage behavior that is rational at both the individual and the social levels.

It is to the establishment of these policies and institutions that we should direct our attention if we are concerned with environmental quality and efficient resource use. Although an environmentally sensitive culture cannot guarantee that decision makers will be sensitive to the environment, it can surely help to establish the appropriate institutions.

12. Aldo Leopold, *A Sand County Almanac and Sketches from Here and There* (Cambridge: Oxford University Press, 1949).

If the goal is to achieve improvements in environmental quality, good intentions are not enough. Like the Montagnais, we should focus on an institutional design with a particular emphasis on property rights since resources owned in common offer perverse incentives that foster overexploitation, inefficiencies, and social conflict. Given the consistently demonstrated behavior of people, we should accept the existence of self-interest and design our institutions accordingly.

Chapter 4

RESOURCE MANAGEMENT IN A BUREAUCRATIC SETTING

As we have seen, some American Indian tribes have historically recognized the importance of property rights in structuring information and incentives and have been innovative and efficient in their management of natural resources. Bureaucrats, on the other hand, do not have transferable property rights to the resources they manage. As a result, even when bureaucrats are highly trained, competent, and well intended, the information and incentives they face do not encourage either sensitive or efficient resource management.

The problem is not one of "bad" or incompetent personnel. Rather, the problem is caused by a reliance on inappropriate institutions that act as a buffer between bureaucratic decision makers and the social consequences of their actions.

Why are natural resources increasingly managed in the public sector? First, there has been a general increase in public sector activity that is not restricted to natural resources. As we move from a society oriented toward productivity to one in which individuals increasingly gain from sensitivity to transfer activity, the scope of government necessarily increases.[1] Second, many important natural resources are difficult to manage privately because of their fugitive nature. Water and air flow and the migratory nature of many birds and wildlife

---

1. See Terry Anderson and Peter J. Hill, *The Birth of a Transfer Society* (Stanford, Calif.: Hoover Institution Press, 1980).

means that property rights can be established only at a high cost. Markets cannot function well without clear and enforceable claims on resource values.

Finally, there is a consistent failure among those who wallow in the affluence of the 1980s to appreciate the constraints and opportunities faced by our ancestors—a relatively poor lot when contrasted with us. Our ancestors were concerned more with wealth creation—a process that generated much of our current well-being— than with preservation. Given nature's bounty (the inventory of natural resources) and the poverty of the average person, the trade-offs they made are understandable. The marginal values of environmental amenities have increased relative to artifactual wealth. Many damn our ancestors for their environmental sins of commission and omission and conclude that bureaucratic management is better now. We maintain, however, that people are still self-interested and that their interests have changed with increased wealth and scarcity.

Partly because of these factors, privately held property rights to natural resources are increasingly attacked. These attacks derive, in part, from what many perceive as an imbalance in the distribution of nature's benefits. In addition, many argue that the pursuit of profits has resulted in irresponsible stewardship of natural resources. Furthermore, many contend that only government control can overcome the negative externalities in the existing market system. As a result of these beliefs, collective decision making has increasingly replaced the rule of willing consent.

This attitude is capsulized by the position that preferences expressed in and by the market are often wrong. The intellectual violence directed at individual freedom by such an elitist view is matched only by its ignorance of historical precedent. A depressingly long list of public sector failures has been generated by such innocent and well-meaning perceptions. The belief that market choices are often incorrect creates more difficulties for its advocates than does the inequity they perceive. Their remedy is often more toxic than the imagined disease.

In pointing to certain market failures, many have denounced the market mechanism as incapable of providing competent resource management.[2] Yet markets, based on voluntary exchange and utiliz-

---

2. This discussion of markets and imperfect property rights has drawn from arguments presented in John Baden and Richard Stroup, "The Environmental Costs of Government Action," *Policy Review* 4 (Spring 1978): 23–24.

ing prices that represent condensed information and incentives, do move resources to their most highly valued uses, provided that transaction costs are negligible and that clear, readily enforceable property rights prevail. Under such circumstances, the market, given the existing distribution of income, will provide the socially optimal production of goods and services. Thus, it is not the market system per se that has led to inefficient resource use. Rather, the very imperfect property rights associated with some natural resources, such as air and water, have hampered efficient and equitable resource allocation. Without clearly defined and enforceable property rights, these resources tend to be underpriced, and negative externalities abound.

The public good and common pool nature of many environmental goods inhibits efficient private market utilization of such resources. Nuisance laws could, in principle, mitigate some of the negative externality effects associated with the use of public good and common pool resources by permitting individuals to collect damages through the courts. However, this mechanism is insufficient because transaction costs among many disparate individuals are extremely high. Individuals have an incentive to avoid legal action, while continuing to enjoy any benefits that might arise from others' efforts to reduce, for example, pollution through court proceedings. This "free rider" problem has induced many to look to mandatory government regulation as a remedy, thereby undermining the rule of willing consent.

No doubt governmental regulation and control can generate some benefits. Reliance on such solutions, however, entirely overlooks the environmental degradation generated by the positive action of government agencies. If the source of all environmental problems derives from profit-seeking individuals or firms operating under market conditions, government bureaucrats whose salaries bear little or no relation to profit are presumed to be free of these incentives to engage in environmentally destructive practices. Yet it is not the profit motive that has resulted in poor resource management. Rather, poorly defined and enforced property rights have generated faulty signals regarding the value of resource inputs which, in turn, have led to inefficient resource management.

The same flaw afflicts government decisionmaking: authority and responsibility are separated. In the private sector, this separation of authority from responsibility ensues when property rights are imperfect. Thus, the factory owner uses a river for free waste removal, paying nothing for that use either in initial costs or subsequent damages to third parties. The owner captures benefits but not costs.

This separation of authority and responsibility is even more wide-spread in the public sector, where those who make policy decisions do not bear all the costs of those decisions. Members of the Federal Power Commission receive support for keeping natural gas wellhead prices low. However, they are not criticized for any environmental damages that have materialized in the wake of increased electricity production, coal conversion to natural gas, or the construction of a multimillion dollar Alaskan gas pipeline, all of which were promoted by their decisions. Even when commissioners are blamed, their individual costs don't approach the total costs to society of their actions.

In the public sector everyone's property is essentially no one's property. The tragedy of the commons described by Garrett Hardin in a nongovernmental setting is particularly applicable to government resource control.[3] Furthermore, in order to prevent the logic of the commons from unfolding too quickly, decision makers restrict and control public use of its resources, transforming so-called public ownership into state ownership. A few benefit at a cost to all the rest as government officials use their authority and the public's funds to regulate the use of public resources.

To claim that representative democracy permits a full and equal sharing of public costs and benefits is simply wrong. Relatively few benefit from federal water projects, artificially low natural gas prices, the chaining of pinyon-juniper stands, or even the preservation of wilderness recreation areas. All, however, pay the costs of poor resource management by the public sector. Those who argue that government control at least provides more equitable influence over decisions than the marketplace are equally mistaken. The "ability to influence government is probably no more (and arguably less) equally distributed than the money income that can influence market decisions."[4]

Though special interest groups receive disproportionate government benefits because of their immense political power, it is not evil individuals that have prompted this inequity. The system's institutional setting, its fundamental structure, best explains this inefficient and inequitable resource management. The same people who nearly destroyed the buffalo population posed no threat to the more valuable beef cattle raised on the western range. In that instance, more clearly defined property rights resulted in the proliferation of beef

3. Garrett Hardin, "The Tragedy of the Commons," *Science* 162 (1968): 1243–48.
4. Baden and Stroup, "The Environmental Costs of Government Action," p. 25.

cattle while the imperfect, if not altogether absent, property rights to the buffalo led to its near elimination. Better institutional arrangements can provide incentives that channel the efforts of imperfect men into productive and efficient, rather than destructive, activities.

Using the property rights paradigm and public choice theory, why should we question the ability of collective management to protect our resources or reflect public desires in a balanced fashion? Is the logic of this paradigm reflected in reality? Does collective management, in fact, promote problems rather than solutions? Finally, what analytical foundations might underlie the development of private institutions and the revision of public institutions to foster efficient, noncoercive management of natural resources?

Before we answer these questions, however, it is useful to examine a common misconception about bureaucratic input into resource management situations. This misconception is that the presence of market externalities is sufficient to guarantee that governmental resource allocation, if carried out by honest, competent public servants, will be superior.

THE FRAMEWORK OF ANALYSIS

The appropriate focus in analyzing public sector behavior is the individual decision maker.[5] It is the individual bureaucrat, the professional public servant, who makes most of the decisions about governmental operations. The average citizen plays little part in this process. Though altruism may sometimes guide bureaucratic behavior, self-interest generally influences the bureaucrat's decision no less than other individuals. Salary, position in the bureaucracy, amount of discretionary budget control, workplace amenities, and office perquisites all contribute to the bureaucrat's well-being. If an agency is expanding its budget and authority, these components of the bureaucrat's welfare improve also. On the other hand, a decrease in the agency's size and budget are generally accompanied by fewer benefits to the bureaucrat. Thus, bureaucrats face strong incentives to increase their agencies' authority and areas of responsibility.[6]

5. The framework of analysis was first developed in ibid., p. 26.
6. For variations on this theme, see T. C. Borcherding, ed., *Budgets and Bureaucrats: The Sources of Government Growth* (Durham, N.C.: Duke University Press, 1977); R. B. McKenzie and Gordon Tullock, *Modern Political Economy* (New York: McGraw-Hill, 1978); and W. A. Niskanen Jr., *Bureaucracy and Representative Government* (Chicago: Aldine-Atherton, 1971).

Unconstrained by the need to generate profits, bureaucrats may ignore or exaggerate the economic efficiency of the projects they administer. The bureaucratic entrepreneur must only arouse sufficient support from a specific clientele that will benefit from the proposed activity. That support, translated into political influence, can result in the necessary congressional appropriation of tax money to finance the action. For the bureaucrat, the tax base is essentially a common pool resource ripe for exploitation.

Few checks exist to shackle bureaucratic discretion and its abuse because voters cannot monitor or influence bureaucratic decision making. Voters are rationally ignorant, not out of apathy, but because acquiring the necessary information to analyze bureaucratic decisions is costly relative to the impact such knowledge provides the individual (see chapter 2).[7] For example, whether pinyon-juniper stands will be inefficiently and destructively chained is normally beyond the individual's control. Thus, the time required to learn about Bureau of Land Management or Forest Service policy may be better spent acquiring information about situations more amenable to one individual's influence.

If government agencies were required to meet standards of economic efficiency, many of their environmentally destructive practices would not occur. In the absence of such standards, the American taxpayer is, in effect, subsidizing the destruction of the environment and enhancing the welfare of bureaucrats and special interests.

Many would benefit from a reduction of government resource control, including taxpayers who currently finance government mismanagement of resources, environmentalists who seek less destruction of scarce resources, and those who simply wish to enjoy more individual freedom. Certainly the growth of government, whatever its benefits, may constitute a serious and unavoidable threat to freedom.

Subconsciously or not, the bureaucrat often seeks to legitimize an implicit subsidy that will benefit a special interest. The beneficiaries of such transfers join in this raid on the common pool resource of taxes generated through and legitimized by the coercive power of the state. Arguably, the size of such a subsidy may depend on its lack of explicitness or quantifiability. If so, the lack of information caused by the absence of market prices benefits both bureau-

---

7. Rational ignorance and other problems of collective decision making are discussed in James Gwartney and Richard Stroup, *Economics: Private and Public Choice,* 2d ed. (New York: Academic Press, 1980); and in McKenzie and Tullock, *Modern Political Economy.*

crats and their special interest clientele. Thus, strong vested interests that control rights to valuable resources have incentives to avoid the reality checks of market pricing tests. Unlike private individuals or firms faced with an accurate price reflection of the value of their inputs, bureaucrats have no check on overuse of resources tapped or paid for from a common pool.

GOOD INTENTIONS, POOR RESULTS

The following review illustrates the dramatic negative externalities that can result from public sector resource control. Each example helps to explode the widespread belief that negative externalities are absent in bureaucratic resource management.

Uneconomic Forest Harvests

The Forest Service administers vast areas of timberland in the western United States. Some of this timberland, notably in northern California and western Oregon and Washington, is extremely productive— the forest equivalent of Iowa cornland. In contrast, the land in the Rocky Mountain states is more productive for recreational and aesthetic uses than for growing trees as a crop. Silvicultural treatments, such as clear-cutting, on many of these high, dry, and ecologically fragile sites often destroy other forest values. In essence, there are trade-offs between timber management and management for other valued uses. In the less productive regions, much of this timber has a *negative value* as commercial timber. The resources used to harvest the timber are often worth more than the timber harvested, even when discounting to zero the value of other uses foregone. It is only because this process is so heavily subsidized that massive ecological disturbances are undertaken.[8]

---

8. See Barney Dowdle, "An Institutional Dinosaur with an Ace: Or, How to Piddle Away Public Timber Wealth and Foul the Environment in the Process," in *Bureaucracy vs. Environment*, ed. John Baden and Richard L. Stroup (Ann Arbor: University of Michigan Press, 1981), pp. 170–85.

Grazing Without Reality Checks

In addition to forest lands, the West possesses vast areas of grazing land, much of it administered by the Bureau of Land Management (BLM). The productivity of this land is so low that it commonly takes from ten to forty or more acres to carry a cow with calf for a month. Relatively large investments in fencing, water development, and seeding can increase the forage productivity of the land, thus expanding the possible number of animal unit months.

The BLM has advocated rest-rotation grazing for this purpose.[9] Under this system, a grazing allotment is fenced into three or four pastures. The first pasture is intensively grazed during the entire period, the second is grazed after forage grasses have gone to seed, and the third is rested. Since the same number of livestock is kept on the allotment as was kept prior to fencing, nearly all of the vegetation in the grazed pastures will be consumed.

Rest-rotation grazing can lead to a number of potentially harmful environmental effects. For example, because the grazed pastures are overstocked, soil compaction becomes a problem, leading to sheet erosion and less watershed protection. When previously open rangeland is fenced, the movement of big game animals is restricted and mortality rates increase. Further, if the program works, shrubs are largely replaced by grasses, and deer, sage grouse, and other species dependent on shrubs may be severely affected.

Although in some locations rest-rotation grazing may indeed improve the range, the outcome is uncertain at best. Because this management practice is relatively capital- and management-intensive, however, only in a few cases or under the most optimistic of assumptions can it be expected to pay its own way. The massive subsidies necessary to transform these rangelands provide a clear example of governmental assistance being required for the economically inefficient modification of environments.

Irrigation

Production and development on much of the land of the western United States is limited by availability of water. Much agricultural

9. See Sabine Kremp, "A Perspective on BLM Grazing Policy," in *Bureaucracy vs. Environment*, pp. 124–53.

land in the West is marginal or uncertain in the absence of irrigation, making possible large social benefits through the development of irrigation systems. However, there is a trade-off between preserving the wild and scenic character of rivers in the West or developing them with dams and irrigation canals. Only rarely can a river have both. Clearly, those who stand to benefit from irrigation water will tend to favor development.

In the public sector, any program that charges Peter to pay Paul will have Paul's support. Consider also the first law of demand, which says that more is demanded at a lower price. Although irrigation water is valuable to those who use it, when the marginal cost to users equals or exceeds its marginal value to them demand will cease. But governmental subsidies of water developments distort the prices irrigators face, and the quantity of water demanded is much higher than it would be in the absence of subsidies. Because the interests of irrigators are concentrated and they are easily organized into potent political groups they can exert tremendous political pressure to convert wild and scenic rivers to dammed and developed ones.

Grazing Revisited

The absence of private property rights and the substitution of direct governmental action have produced innumerable other instances of adverse environmental or conservation conditions. For example, overgrazing of the western Great Plains by cattlemen on public lands destroyed the fragile ecological balance of the grasslands, preparing the way for the dust bowl. Without the extension of private property rights into this area, each stockman was driven by economic incentives to overgraze before someone else did, to run more stock than the land could sustain through time, and to graze too early in the year before the young grasses matured and seeded. Nor was there any incentive for any user to reseed overgrazed areas or to attempt any form of irrigation. Similar conditions still prevail on BLM lands where cattlemen and sheepmen can graze their animals on land they do not own (and may not be able to use the next year) at fees below what they would pay on private land. Under these conditions, they have an incentive to overgraze.[10]

10. See ibid.

Land and fresh water are not the only resources threatened by this tragedy of the commons. Most of the world's oceans fall into a similar category. With the absence of private ownership of most of the fishery resources, including fish, shellfish, and whales, one species after another has been overharvested because no individual user has had any economic incentive to preserve them. This situation can be contrasted with the rational conservation practices carried out in private fishing operations.[11]

Destroying Pinyon-Juniper

The Forest Service and the BLM have removed pinyon and juniper trees from thousands of acres of public lands in the southern Rocky Mountain states. Generally, trees are cleared by chaining, a process whereby two D-8–size crawler tractors (85,000 pounds and over) are connected by up to 600 feet of anchor chain (weighing as much as 120 pounds per link) and are driven parallel through the woodlands. Herbicides, burning, and "tree crushers" are sometimes used on smaller areas. The Forest Service estimates that approximately 400,000 acres in Utah and Nevada are "suitable for rehabilitation" (potential grazing land) by such clearing at a projected rate of from 10,000 to 13,000 acres per year. The trees are killed, and the debris is burned or left.[12]

Removing trees that consume space, light, water, and nutrients can foster the growth of more feed for livestock. If the value of the additional feed exceeds the costs of producing it (including externalities as costs or benefits) and if those who reap the benefits are willing to pay the costs, this program might be justifiable despite its assault on our ecological sensitivities. But this is not the case. There is little evidence that the practice has net positive benefits. Although improved wildlife habitat provides one justification for chaining, "a summary conclusion for the several million acres of treated P-J [pinyon-juniper] is one of no overall impact — either positive

11. See James W. Wilson, "A Test of the Tragedy of the Commons," in *Managing the Commons*, ed. Garrett Harden and John Baden (San Francisco: W. H. Freeman, 1977), pp. 96–111.

12. Ronald M. Lanner, "Chained to the Bottom," in *Bureaucracy vs. Environment*, pp. 154–69.

or negative."[13] A similar finding holds for purported watershed improvements.

Though chaining does increase forage for livestock, its cost appears to exceed the value of the additional forage. Even though ranchers (who make up a small proportion of the U.S. population) reap subsidized gains from the practice, there is a significant social loss. Reviewing agency reports on the subject, Ronald M. Lanner has noted that a "careful reading of environmental statements . . . will disclose them to be documents of advocacy. They are not balanced weighings of evidence, but necessary props placed in support of an ongoing agency program."[14]

Forest Service and BLM decision makers do not intentionally harm the environment. Initially, experts hypothesized that chaining would produce benefits, and we assume that the practice was undertaken in good faith. Eventually, chaining became an important part of many district budgets, and the incentives to reevaluate its impact realistically are negative, illustrating the tendency of governmental programs to persist and expand. In the private sector, sunken costs are just that—sunk. Given the politics of the budgetary process in the public sector, however, sunken costs become "investments" that can yield a return in the form of additional funds.

If bureaucrats are well intentioned and sincerely want to improve agency performance, they must advance in the organization. But advancement in a bureaucracy is normally not achieved by advocating positions that lead to budget cuts. Thus, persons seeking to advance the public interest are locked into a perverse system whose incentives tend to perpetuate practices like chaining.

A Startling Example: Cooperation versus Competition

Ten miles south of Intercoastal City, Louisiana, lie 26,800 acres of marshland owned by the Audubon Society.[15] The society operates

13. Ted Terrel and J. Juan Spillett, "Pinyon-Juniper Conversion: Its Impact on Mule Deer and Other Wildlife," in *The Pinyon-Juniper Ecosystem: A Symposium*, ed. Gerald F. Gifford and Frank E. Busby (Logan: Utah State University, 1975), pp. 105–19.

14. Ronald M. Lanner, "The Eradication of Pinyon-Juniper Woodland," *Western Wildlands* (Spring 1977), p. 17.

15. For more on this, see John Baden and Richard Stroup, "Saving the Wilderness," *Reason* 13 (July 1981): 28–36.

the land as a wildlife sanctuary for deer, armadillo, muskrat, otter, and mink. The Rainey Wildlife Sanctuary is also home to more than fifty thousand snow geese. In addition, the Rainey Sanctuary is also the site of natural gas well platforms and private cattle herds. Gas wells and cattle herds in terrain managed by professional, dedicated environmentalists may seem totally out of place. But even though the aims of developers and environmentalists may seem to conflict, their cooperation on the Rainey Preserve has been beneficial for all— including the geese. Unfettered by the heavy hand of the bureaucrat, the market has worked its magic to benefit two very different interests. In the environment of free exchange, all interests have an incentive to recognize and accommodate trade-offs.

The Nature Conservancy, another environmental group, has joined the move to private cooperation and ownership. The group buys and manages ecologically sensitive areas and has done so for more than thirty years. As a recent fund raiser emphasized, "We don't sue or picket or preach. We simply do our best to locate, scientifically, those spots on earth where something wild and rare and beautiful is thriving or hanging on precariously. Then we buy them. We're good at it." For example, at the Mile Hi-Ramsey Canyon Preserve in Arizona, the Nature Conservancy pays for the maintenance of the area by providing lodging, pet boarding, and tours—for a price. This arrangement has not led to any damage to the environment and has allowed the Nature Conservancy to continue its efforts to preserve ecologically sensitive and valuable land. The same group also donates some of its land to the government. Having paid the piper it can call the tune and specify future management practices.

Under the proper institutional arrangements land can be managed for the benefit of all. With well-defined, transferable property rights, all interested parties have the incentive to move resources to more highly valued uses—in order to maintain or increase the value of the land. When one party gives up a value to the other, compensation is paid. All such factors are seriously weighed by both sides before a decision is made. This self-interest has led to the successful and profitable cooperation exhibited In the Rainey Preserve and on Nature Conservancy land.

FRAMEWORK FOR BETTER
RESOURCE MANAGEMENT

According to the property rights paradigm, environmental problems in a market setting occur when imperfect property rights to a resource prevail, thus distorting resource prices. Without clear, enforceable property rights, those with decision-making authority are not held responsible for all of their actions. Relinquishing private rights and the rule of willing consent in favor of collective action will actually create rather than resolve environmental problems. Even with good intentions and expertise, public servants are likely to generate environmental problems because they lack the feedback and reality checks inherent in the price system and markets.

The search for the means of improving our management of natural resources requires three steps.[16] First, the real problem must be identified: it is the separation of authority from personal responsibility, all too prevalent in the private sector and virtually universal in the public sector, that inhibits accountability. Second, we must accept an imperfect solution. Though markets are imperfect, their failures do not automatically imply that collective action is better. An imperfect market may, in fact, represent the best possible alternative. Finally, our institutions must be restructured to provide the incentives and information for more efficient resource management.

---

16. Of course, the opposite is also true: an imperfection in collective management should not automatically cause us to avoid governmental action. The grass is *not* always greener. The fate of the environment under a collectivist system has been explored in three studies: Fred Singleton, ed., *Environmental Misuse in the Soviet Union* (New York: Praeger, 1976); Philip R. Pryde, *Conservation in the Soviet Union* (New York: Cambridge University Press, 1973); and Marshall I. Goldman, *The Spoils of Progress: Environmental Pollution in the Soviet Union* (Cambridge, Mass.: The MIT Press, 1972). These books have been reviewed by Robert J. Smith in *Policy Review* (Fall 1977).

Chapter 5

ENERGY SCARCITIES AND POLITICAL OPPORTUNISM[1]

Vilhjalmur Stefansson, noted arctic explorer, ethnologist, and director of the Arctic Institute until his death at ninety-two, has shown that North American Eskimos were especially gifted in creating myths.[2] One tribe, for example, held that there was a group of men— just out of reach of visual inspection—who grew antlers and dined on human flesh. Such myths are highly creative, great fun to contemplate, and usually harmless. Unlike these myths, however, those that surround America's energy situation, can be extraordinarily dangerous.

People continue to believe that optimizing social welfare requires active governmental participation. This belief persists despite our country's extensive and disappointing experience with government management. It is commonly believed that private individuals cannot be trusted to manage energy resources. Because of characteristics inherent in energy systems, optimizing social welfare requires active governmental management, coordination, and investment. A distrust of voluntary exchanges among persons pursuing their own self-interest continues to feed this myth.

1. For a further discussion of energy regulation, see the Pacific Institute volumes by David Glasner entitled, *Politics, Prices, and Petroleum. The Political Economy of Energy* (Cambridge, Mass.: Ballinger, 1983), and by John Moorhouse entitled *Electric Utility Regulation and the Energy Crisis* (Cambridge, Mass.: Ballinger, forthcoming).
2. Vilhjalmur Stefansson, *My Life with the Eskimo* (New York: Macmillan, 1913).

Yet more than two centuries ago Adam Smith explained why individuals in a market setting generally act as if they had the interests of others in mind.[3] Individuals engaging in voluntary exchange to improve their own well-being will naturally move resources to more highly valued uses, thus benefiting others. "Self-interest is a powerful motivator, and voluntary exchange (the market mechanism) harnesses that powerful force for the good of all who wish to participate in the economy."[4] Government regulations, taxation, and subsidies superimposed on markets distort that process.

THE ROLE OF SELF-INTEREST AND GOVERNMENT

Nearly all governments transfer resources and protect the interests of some against others, rendering efforts to control the relevant units of government among the most profitable activities available to individuals, even though such individual gains often come at a net cost to society. To the degree that government controls and directs the economy, rent seeking becomes increasingly attractive.[5] Rational ignorance and the special interest effect guarantee this result in democratic countries that systematically and substantially intervene in the economy (see chapter 2).[6]

The original U.S. Constitution was unique in its establishment of institutions that (1) made it cumbersome and costly to generate resource transfers through government activity and (2) permitted individuals to profit by moving resources to more highly valued uses. These institutions provided a framework for encouraging productiv-

3. Adam Smith, *The Wealth of Nations*, ed. Edwin Cannon, 2 vols. (Chicago: University of Chicago Press, 1976). Originally published in 1904 by Methuen & Co.

4. John Baden and Richard Stroup, "Entrepreneurship, Energy, and the Political Economy of Hope," *Proceedings of the Southwestern Legal Foundation Annual Institute* 19 (San Francisco: Matthew Bender, 1981): 337. See also, generally, Richard Stroup and John Baden, "Responsible Individuals and the Nation's Energy Future," *Cato Journal* 1 (Fall 1981): 421–38.

5. This point was developed from a seminal article by Anne O. Krueger, "The Political Economy of the Rent Seeking Society," *American Economic Review* 64 (June 1974): 291–303. The historical development of rent seeking in the United States is traced by Terry Anderson and Peter J. Hill in *The Birth of a Transfer Society* (Stanford, Calif.: Hoover Institution Press, 1980).

6. James Gwartney and Richard Stroup, *Economics: Private and Public Choice*, 2d ed. (New York: Academic Press, 1980), chap. 4.

ity and expanding the welfare of individuals. Unfortunately, the institutions were susceptible to the pressures of organized interests pushing for government policies to benefit them at the expense of others. Given this susceptibility, it is rational for interest groups to vie for influence over government policies, striving to have programs implemented that benefit their particular interests. Though such policies may benefit the particular groups that have lobbied for them, they generally reduce overall efficiency, producing a net loss to the general public.

The world is populated by self-interested individuals constantly seeking ways to make themselves better off. If the highest payoffs are obtained by using the coercive power of government, investments to acquire this power will materialize. A crisis, such as increasing energy scarcity, coupled with the "right" set of beliefs can foster the expansion of governmental control. Expanding the management role of government increases incentives for investing in political activities rather than engaging in productive activities. Productivity suffers as entrepreneurial talent is squandered and individual freedom is reduced.

HISTORY OF ENERGY REGULATION

The oil crisis of October 1973 aroused increasing demands by many Americans for a coherent energy policy. The political left, distrusting the foresight and self-discipline of the average American, sought controls over energy use. Such distrust is behind legislation for automobile mileage standards, the fifty-five-mile-per-hour speed limit, and thermostat controls in buildings, among other policies forcing conservation on the American public. The political right, believed to be less enthusiastic about conservation controls, has also called for government controls to ensure sufficient supplies of strategic resources. Contending that individuals place too little emphasis on national security matters when making decisions in the market, they fear that energy supplies and reserves may become too small. The necessity for military and economic preparedness has thus become the excuse advanced in behalf of more government controls.

However, the increase of governmental control, especially in times of a fuel shortage or other emergency, works strongly against the private alternative. Reviewing energy regulation over the past quarter century in the United States can help illuminate our current status and lay the groundwork for understanding political economic dilemmas in the energy field.

Meaningful interference by governmental institutions was first forcefully demonstrated by the Federal Power Commission (FPC) in 1954 when it began fixing the wellhead price of natural gas. Until 1961, when the FPC adopted the Permian Basin method of setting rates based on the average historical costs of production in an area, the commission used a case-by-case approach to establish wellhead prices that reflected production costs.[7] This approach had two negative market effects. First, fixed prices caused unprofitability of all but the most easily accessible gas deposits. As a result, exploration was dramatically retarded and production dropped. Second, the real price of natural gas declined relative to market-determined prices of energy alternatives, leading to sharp increases in natural gas usage.

Oil production and pricing were also affected by regulatory market intervention. In 1954 producers successfully argued for and received protection from "cheap" oil in the form of import restrictions. The secondary effect of this action was the initiation of a "drain America first" policy on domestic oil and a rapid drop in price for international crude oil. Then, in 1960, the Organization of Petroleum Exporting Countries (OPEC) was formed. Incentives for exploration abroad were reduced in the face of lower relative prices of foreign oil, and the greater use of domestic, "protected" oil led to depleted U.S. reserves. The stage was set for OPEC's successful price increase strategy that began in 1973.

Compounding the pending energy crisis were two events, both of which worsened the impact of future boycotts: the initiation of inefficient forms of pollution controls and OPEC price increases. Beginning in the late 1960s, the United States initiated direct and universal pollution emission standards that greatly reduced the mileage ratings of average automobiles. In addition, Congress eliminated the long-time implicit subsidy given to refiners in the form of unpriced and unrestricted air and water pollution. Rather than increasing user fees or pollution taxes to optimize the use of these resources, refineries were penalized and were unable to obtain new construction permits for capacity expansions. Demand for oil products rose, and production and refinery capacity dropped.

7. Ibid., p. 664.

The creation of the Department of Energy (originally the Federal Energy Office) also contributed to the energy crisis. It is now generally conceded that the DOE's entitlement allocation programs, pricing policies, and other assorted "crisis" measures compounded the growing misinformation in the energy resource market and the disincentives for exploration and production.

A brief look at government's response to the externality problems of a common pool resource demonstrates that policymakers understood that there are maximum, efficient rates for the extraction of petroleum resources. Such rates were administered by some state agencies, but the ignorance of opportunity costs caused by fiat pricing (and political pressures from well owners) led to oil prices being sustained above market equilibrium levels for years. In effect, those agencies exercised monopoly power on the behalf of oil producers.

Related pricing problems emerged in 1973 after OPEC "shut off the tap." Governmental regulators—led by a so-called energy czar—failed to consider the lengthy production cycle for petroleum, the benefits from which are only now being realized. Further, a critical lack of understanding of the distinction between proven reserves (those recoverable at *current* prices and levels of technology) and absolute reserves (the total in existence) led to hysterical predictions of total oil depletion within fifteen years.

An additional price consideration works against misconceptions about governmental intervention. One effect of OPEC's price increases in the face of the short-run inelasticity in supply was to plant the seeds for economically viable conservation and alternative sources in the longer run. The trend toward better home insulation, greater automobile mileage, and thousands of related adjustments to higher energy prices continues today.

DIVERSITY IN BIOLOGICAL AND ECONOMIC SYSTEMS

Biologists are among the few who appreciate the beneficial consequences of diversity. In a constantly changing world, the probability of survival is enhanced when uniformity is incomplete. A gene pool is more likely to survive if the variety among its carriers increases the odds of some individuals surviving environmental change. Essentially, evolution is the gradual adaptation to trends in environmental change.

In the world studied by biologists, monocultures in a given location are notoriously fragile and short-lived.[8] Although there are questions about this view, uniformity in human society is likely to limit the possibilities for adaptation to change.

Innovations within economic systems represent the functional equivalent of mutations in biotic systems. As long as innovators face the full costs of their efforts, a society interested in increased productivity should encourage innovative activity. In an economic setting, successful experimentation quickly generates change, for there are strong incentives to emulate success.

Innovations in energy development are essential in determining our energy future, but whether such innovations will materialize is uncertain. Will potential innovators be permitted to experiment? Will markets be available for energy innovations, particularly if government subsidies and regulations distort resource markets? Will innovators be able to obtain funding for their ventures? Answers to these questions depend largely on how innovative activity is handled. If energy innovations develop in the marketplace, the innovators need only convince a few investors that a particular idea is worth pursuing. On the other hand, if innovations are promoted through the political process, a majority of the political representatives must be convinced of a project's merits. Such a process inevitably discourages innovative activity relative to the marketplace, where all sorts of wild schemes can be financed. In a democratic setting in which majority approval for funding is required, the potential for successful innovation is clearly restricted. The same is true in a representative democracy, unless a powerful special interest group pushes the innovation. In this case, even bad innovations may be funded.

Governmental policies may stifle demand for innovation in addition to suppressing innovation itself. Nowhere has this process been more evident than in the production of energy. In the large and diverse market of the United States, wind, hydroelectric power, and wood alcohol all were once in great demand in various locations.[9]

---

8. For a dissenting view from a noted ecologist, see Paul Colinvaux, *Why Big Fierce Animals Are Rare: An Ecologist's Perspective* (Princeton, N.J.: Princeton University Press, 1979), esp. chap. 10; idem, *Introduction to Ecology* (New York: John Wiley and Sons, 1973).

9. See, for example, F. Culver, "Performance of Two Successful Windmill Generating Plants," *Electrical World* 69 (February 1917): 367–69; K. Frederick, "Can We Put the Sun to Work?" *Scientific American* 115 (7 October 1916): 329; A. Ingalls, "Power from the

Interest in fuel alcohol eventually waned, probably because of the declining price of gasoline. Wind and hydroelectric power suffered a similar fate. But demand for these two energy sources, once widely used in remote rural areas far from the cheap power provided by central generating stations, did not succumb to market forces. Instead, federal subsidies of electricity to rural power customers ultimately almost eliminated any demand for these alternative energy sources.

The Rural Electrification Administration

In order to make power available at an artificially low price to rural residents, the Rural Electrification Administration (REA) arranged low interest, guaranteed loans, subsidized expertise, and granted exemption from income taxes to rural power cooperatives. Rural customers who otherwise might have been customers for alternative sources of power were thus subsidized in their use of central station electricity. Rate regulation provided additional subsidies to all customers of electric utilities. Electricity has thus been made available to rural residents at the same rate that it is available to residents of more densely populated areas, even though the latter are much cheaper to serve. The result has been the demise of some alternative energy markets, as well as a loss of national resiliency. Just as a biological monoculture may be less likely than a biologically diverse community to withstand environmental shocks, a monotechnological society is certainly more prone to serious danger from external shocks. The economic diversity fostered by free markets is a healthy state of affairs. Unfortunately, governmental activities often inhibit innovation and diversity.

Gasahol: A Study in Induced Innovation

Government subsidies not only stifle diversity, they also make possible whole new industrial developments, barren of the cost or per-

<hr>

Wind," *The Scientific American Digest* 134 (February 1926): 114–15; F. Shuman, "Feasibility of Utilizing Power from the Sun," *Scientific American* 110 (February 1914): 179; and M. A. Replogle, "Hydraulic Power Plant at Henry Ford Farms," *Power* 43 (4 January 1916).

formance improvements needed for market success. All that is required to promote such undertakings is an organized lobbying effort
on behalf of resource owners favored by the new program.

The farm lobby, for example, has diverted many tax dollars into
their program to use grain in the production of ethanol. Gasahol, a
mixture of 10 percent ethanol and 90 percent gasoline, can stretch
our gasoline supplies. The process is so expensive, however, that
some agricultural economists have compared it to stretching our supplies of hamburger by grinding a few extra pounds of tenderloin
steak.

Politically powerful grain interests have promoted and received
gasoline tax exemptions at the state and federal levels and an implicit
subsidy from the entitlement program. These subsidies cost more,
per gallon of ethanol, than the total cost per gallon of producing
gasoline from expensive OPEC crude. In addition, the farmers have
arranged for a 10 percent investment tax credit on top of the normal
tax credit for facilities that produce ethanol from grain. Political
power, not economic efficiency—or even commonly held notions of
equity—determine such collectively made decisions.

ALTERNATIVE ENERGY AND
MARKET FAILURE

Are proposed governmental subsidies for the expansion of energy
supplies justifiable in terms of either social welfare or economic efficiency? How has the belief that the domestic energy industry is in
need of financial assistance developed? Why would profit-seeking
capitalists fail to invest in the development of alternative energy systems? There is an obvious answer: such investments seem unlikely to
generate satisfactory profits. Such systems simply cost more than
they are worth.

Until October 1973, the real price of conventional fossil fuels was
declining, and the percentage of decrease was increasing annually.
Obviously, such a market inhibits the development of substitute
energy sources. The shortage of the mid-1970s was caused by political rather than physical factors. Consequently, standard models of
resource consumption could not have predicted it, nor could investors, entrepreneurs, and speculators have been expected to buffer
effectively the consumer from the impacts of shortages. If even a few

well-financed speculators had foreseen the price increase, it would have been smoothed out by speculative activities.

In response to the energy problems of the 1970s many believe that the government should subsidize synthetic fuel and alternative energy programs. But government allocation of resources distorts market signals, and resources flow to those with the most political power rather than directly to those consumers desiring them most. Why should a private company invest in wind or solar power when the government is paying its competitors' costs in synthetic fuel production?

Individuals make investments in the private sector only if the benefits projected by the most optimistic investors exceed the costs. When the government subsidizes alternative energy sources, energy costs are borne by society through taxation rather than paid for directly by the consumer. As Paul Joskow and Robert Pindyck wrote, "Americans would in fact be much worse off with higher taxes than with higher energy prices. Individuals can choose to avoid paying higher energy prices by limiting their consumption, but they have no choice regarding the taxes they must pay." [10]

Subsidies to encourage energy production by the private sector are unlikely to improve social welfare or economic efficiency. Resources allocated by the market tend to be used more efficiently, flowing toward those uses where they can be put to best advantage. In the absence of governmental intervention, research and development follow their own course—directed toward satisfying consumer demands. In contrast, when subsidies are involved, political power allocates resources. It has yet to be demonstrated that such decisions can optimize social welfare.

Research and Development of Alternative Energy Sources

Three factors may explain the atrophy of research and development in alternative energy systems. First, during the 1920s, substantial economies of scale developed in the production of electricity. When energy production is "too cheap to monitor," the cost of delivery

---

10. Paul Joskow and Robert S. Pindyck, "Those Subsidized Energy Schemes," *Wall Street Journal*, July 2, 1979.

becomes the only relevant cost. With the generation of electricity at a few cents per kilowatt, delivery costs had to be huge before small-scale generators become economically preferable. Furthermore, a new technique had made it increasingly economical to transmit power over long distances. Though these technical considerations partly explain the failure of alternative energy systems to develop, two other factors were decisive.

The politically determined rate structure of electricity has effectively shielded individuals from the consequences of their energy consumption decisions, especially in rural areas. Some users don't pay the real costs of producing and delivering electricity. Consequently, they have too little incentive to conserve or to use resources efficiently given the artificially low prices they pay for electricity use. In some systems, all those using the same amount of electricity actually pay the same amount *regardless of delivery cost.*

If people faced rates that reflected marginal costs, those living in remote and expensive locations would be potential consumers of small-scale energy production units. The continued existence of this market would have encouraged innovation by the many firms that were active in the 1920s, 1930s, and 1940s.

In addition to the politically determined rate structure, another government policy resulting in the creation of the Rural Electrification Administration (REA) undermined the development of alternative energy industries. Established during the 1930s to subsidize power delivery to people in rural areas, the REA provided federally guaranteed 2 percent loans and eliminated income taxes on rural power cooperatives. The taxpayer picked up part of the expensive costs of delivering power to remote rural areas.

President Roosevelt, who created the REA through an executive order, made the following observation on the elasticity of demand for electric energy in 1934: "We are going to see . . . electricity and power made so cheap that they will become a standard article of use, not only for agriculture and manufacturing, but also for every home within reach of an electric light line. The experience of those sections of the world that have cheap power proves very conclusively that the cheaper the power the more of it is used."[11]

11. D. Coyle, *Electric Power on the Farm* (Washington, D.C.: Government Printing Office, 1936).

During the congressional debates preceding the passage of REA legislation, Senator William H. King asked whether there had been any hearings on the bill and, if not, on what information or data the bill had been based. Senator George W. Norris replied:

> The question is a very proper one, but I say to the Senator that we had no hearings in the ordinary sense. I thought there was no necessity of having them. . . . In the first place, so far as I have been able to learn, outside of some private power companies, I know and have heard no objection being made anywhere in regard to the bill. . . . All of the replies we received on the merits of the bill were favorable.[12]

Although REA legislation was enacted in the 1930s, windmills and wind generators survived another twenty years, the time required to string electric wires through the central and western states. Marcellus Jacobs, founder of the once-successful Jacobs Wind Electric Company, asserted that without question the spread of REA-subsidized power facilities signaled the end of his business.[13] In addition, the solar water heating industry, resurging after World War II, was stunted by cheap electric rates.

A Lesson about Subsidy Costs

Though the REA had worthy goals, unanticipated costs clearly accompanied the decision to subsidize power delivery. The inefficient use of power poles, labor, and copper wire is a regrettable but almost trivial cost when compared with the loss of forty years of research and development in alternative energy systems. Subsidized electrical power stifled the market for alternatives, thus eliminating any incentive to produce and develop new products.

Federal subsidies in part inhibited development of alternative energy systems. They should not now be called upon to subsidize the very systems whose demise they fostered. Such subsidies, however well-intentioned, will serve only to inhibit development in competing nonsubsidized areas. Since the future is uncertain, we can never know what the cost of our bias will be. We can only be certain that there will be a cost.

12. Ibid.
13. Wilson Clark, *Energy for Survival* (Garden City, N.J.: Anchor Press, 1974).

Energy, the Residual Claimant,
and Transferability of Rights

The different degrees to which responsibility and authority are linked distinguish private from political sector decision making. Markets with clear, enforceable, and transferable rights make individual decision makers responsible for their actions. The public sector, on the other hand, has no comparable mechanism for ensuring accountability.

Accountability in the public sector is an elusive goal. It is impossible to hold decision makers responsible for the accomplishment of what we cannot, even in theory, establish as the socially appropriate goals. Since socially preferable outcomes cannot be measured or defined in any detail, special interests can be expected to dominate public decisions.

The case of the Bonneville Power Administration (BPA), a federal agency in charge of selling federally owned hydroelectric power in the Pacific Northwest, reveals the costs of not having the residual claimant making decisions on a valuable resource. Because the dams producing the power were built at the best river sites in the Pacific Northwest, their electricity production has a very low cost. At the same time, it has a very high value. Users who do not receive the electricity typically turn to expensive, alternative sources, such as coal-fired or nuclear plants.

Though alternative methods of producing the same electricity are far more expensive, they are currently being undertaken. Yet, the BPA power is sold at accounting cost, largely to huge aluminum plants established many years ago to take advantage of the cheap power. Other users of electricity in the region would pay very high prices to obtain that electricity, but the rights are not transferable. There is no residual claimant to that electricity. Thus we have the spectacle of the BPA delivering electricity to the aluminum plants at about one-fifth of the cost which utilities all over the region must pay for new power.

Could BPA power be conserved by the aluminum industry and some of the power sold to other customers? Technically, considerable conservation could be achieved. At a cost, aluminum plants could be modified to use new processes that consume at least a third less electricity per ingot of aluminum than is currently used. In addition, power-intensive aluminum could be better conserved if users paid the full cost. But since neither the BPA nor their aluminum customers own the electricity and cannot benefit from conserving it at a cost in order to sell it, the conservation and the socially efficient transfers never occur. Those with the authority to implement the desirable changes are not fully responsible for the effects of their decisions. It is easier for them to delay the painful transition—or, more accurately, to force others to make even more costly adjustments.

SNG from Coal

Synthetic natural gas (SNG), as the name implies, is a substitute for natural gas. Small quantities of SNG are currently being produced in the United States from petroleum products. It could be produced from coal, but the costs would be much higher than current natural gas prices. Over the last decade and until deregulation, there was a large and growing shortage of natural gas and a corresponding interest in coal gasification. The process itself, however, is not new.

The history of coal gasification technology dates back to 1670.[14] Probably the most thoroughly proven technology is used in Lurgi units, first developed in Germany over fifty years ago. The Lurgi process combines crushed coal with steam and oxygen under high pressure to make a mixture of hydrogen, hydrocarbons, nitrogen, and carbon oxides. The production of pipeline-quality gas requires that the commercially unproven methanation process be used. This process removes all carbon monoxide and some carbon dioxide and raises the heating value to 900 to 1,000 British thermal units per standard cubic foot (Btu/scf).

Though new technologies are also being explored, the first plants are expected to use the Lurgi process.[15] The negative environmental impacts of coal gasification include problems with coal mining (strip mining in the West), air pollution from the gasification process, and the loss of instream values from streams dewatered to provide feedstock and cooling water.[16]

14. For a history and description of coal gasification technology, see U.S., Department of Interior, Office of Coal Research, *Evaluation of Coal Gasification Technology, Part I: Pipeline Quality Gas* (Washington, D.C.: Government Printing Office, 1973).

15. See ibid., and R. L. Stroup and W. N. Thurman, "Will Coal Gasification Come to the Northern Great Plains?" *Montana Business Quarterly* 14 (Winter 1976): 33-39.

16. Stanley M. Greenfield, "Environmental Problems with Fossil Fuels," *Options for U. S. Energy Policy* (San Francisco: Institute for Contemporary Studies, 1977), pp. 92-103.

The growing shortage of natural gas began in 1971, but its cause can be traced to the Federal Power Commission's (FPC) regulation of wellhead natural gas prices in the 1950s.[17] Because the price of gas was kept below equilibrium, a predictable shortage resulted, compelling some to propose SNG as the solution to the shortage. But the cost of SNG is so great and the movement toward SNG is so tentative that commercial production will probably require governmental support and subsidy.

Among the firms most interested in converting coal to SNG are natural gas utilities and pipeline companies. Both are regulated and both are subject to rate-making processes that make extra profit dependent on extra investment in capital. More natural gas from wells, bought at higher wellhead prices, will simply cause a cost pass-through; but an investment in an SNG plant would allow extra return on the investment. Thus, if the utility can obtain investment capital at a low enough rate—a possibility made likelier by proposed governmental loan guarantees—it can increase its total profit. It is important to retain a rolled-in rate structure, however, wherein SNG could be sold at a lower combined price with natural gas, the price of which is held well below equilibrium by federal regulation. Whether a rolled-in rate structure will be allowed has not been finally settled.[18]

Briefly, three major types of governmental intervention are encouraging SNG production. Federal wellhead price regulation of natural gas, designed to protect the consumer from high prices, caused the shortage that SNG could perhaps reduce. Federal subsidies, both directly to research and demonstration facilities and indirectly via proposed loan guarantees, make coal gasification a less prohibitive investment for private firms. Utility rate regulation often allows average cost pricing and encourages new capital investments, again making SNG more attractive. Without these positive governmental actions, it is unlikely that SNG from coal would be seriously considered outside research laboratories. It simply costs too much at current energy price levels.

17. A history of the Federal Power Commission is found in S. G. Breyer and P. W. Mac-Avoy, *Energy Regulation by the Federal Power Commission* (Washington, D.C.: The Brookings Institution, 1974). See also Ernst R. Habicht Jr., "U.S. Natural Gas Policy: An Autopsy," in *Bureaucracy vs. Environment*, ed. John Baden and Richard L. Stroup (Ann Arbor: University of Michigan Press, 1981), pp. 64–76.

18. See Richard L. Stroup, "The Policy-Induced Demand for Coal Gasification," in *Bureaucracy vs. Environment*, pp. 77–86.

CHALK UP ANOTHER MYTH

The claims for governmental intervention in energy resource markets are based on a series of mistaken beliefs. Like other natural resources, efficient energy resource development can benefit most directly from correct information communicated through market prices. To the extent that regulatory patterns accurately reflect the market, distortions are minimized, but there is little historical evidence that this often happens. Political decisions are efficient only by chance. Efficiency, as such, has no political constituency. Again, negative externalities associated with governmental institutions superseding market actions are likely to exceed the misallocations of their market counterparts.

The long history of governmental intervention in energy markets has been largely motivated by a misguided concern for maintaining "low cost" energy. Exacerbating the problem by smothering innovations of producers and users alike, crowding out energy sources, and demonstrating failures because there is no residual claimant, governmental intervention in energy and energy resource markets has been a notable and consistent failure.

Chapter 6

PROPERTY RIGHTS AND
GROUNDWATER MANAGEMENT*

Over the last several years, more and more people have come to believe that the United States will soon face serious and perhaps debili-
tating shortages of water, especially in the West.[1] As with many
other natural resources, water problems are often discussed in terms
of finite supply versus infinite demand. The media have seized upon
stories of thirsty municipalities and withered farm crops as evidence
that the supply of water may be running low.[2]

Although this belief is popular and has a great deal of public and
private support, in reality there is no long-term shortage of water in
sight. Our present worries have been caused largely by an institutional framework that encourages profligate water use.

An equally false corollary of this belief in an impending water
shortage is that because there is insufficient water for all those who

*This chapter was written by David T. Fractor, Research Associate at the Center for
Political Economy and Natural Resources.

1. For a further discussion of water resources, see the Pacific Institute volume entitled
Water Rights: Scarce Resource Allocation, Bureaucracy, and the Environment, ed. Terry L.
Anderson (Cambridge, Mass.: Ballinger, 1983).

2. T. Y. Canby, "Our Most Precious Resource: Water," *National Geographic* (August
1980), p. 144–79. See also, "In New Mexico, Water Is Valuable Resource–And So Is
Water Boss," *Wall Street Journal*, 1 May 1980; "Huge Area in Midwest Relying on Irrigation
Is Depleting Its Water," *Wall Street Journal*, 6 August 1980; "Small California Towns Say
Los Angeles Policy Is Draining Their Land," *Wall Street Journal*, 4 February 1981; "Water:
Will We Have Enough to Go Around?" *U. S. News and World Report*, 19 June 1981.

want it or need it, government must ensure – through regulation, central control, and management – that remaining supplies are efficiently and equitably distributed.

To demonstrate the falsity of this belief, we will examine the very real problems this nation faces in dealing with water, focusing primarily on our most abundant source of fresh water, groundwater. There is an estimated thirty times as much water beneath the earth's surface as in all freshwater rivers and lakes combined. Approximately one-quarter of the water consumed in the United States and one-half of the drinking water come from underground aquifers. It is important to realize, however, that 26 percent of the 82 billion gallons of groundwater used daily is overdraft (that is, long-term use in excess of natural replenishment, or recharge). In other words, the groundwater stock in the United States is falling by 21 billion gallons a day.

Groundwater is especially important in areas where surface supplies are limited or highly variable, as in the western United States. Comprising 60 percent of the land area of the forty-eight contiguous states, the West receives only 25 percent of the precipitation. As a result, the problem of groundwater overdraft has become especially acute in this region. As groundwater supplies have disappeared, previously irrigated farms in west Texas have switched to growing less productive dryland crops. Sinkholes have appeared in Florida. Sections of the San Joaquin Valley in central California have dropped by as much as twenty-eight feet because of a prolonged overdraft of the underlying groundwater basins.[3] Given these problems, groundwater management in the West might reasonably be expected to ensure efficient use and distribution. As we will see, however, this is not the case.

Can we expect groundwater to be efficiently allocated in the absence of rules and regulations regarding its use? Probably not. Groundwater is often found in underground pools or aquifers so large that more than one user can have access to it. This is a classic example of a common pool where, with unrestricted use, the actions of one user are likely to adversely affect all other users.

The decision on whether to pump groundwater depends on three things: (1) the value of the water, (2) extraction costs, and (3) how much water remains in the aquifer. Under strictly common pool conditions where no one owns specific rights to any portion of the sup-

---

3. "The Browning of America," *Newsweek*, 23 February 1981, pp. 26–37.

ply, the incentives for groundwater use are as follows: First, the water will be pumped as rapidly as possible, since waiting until the next period, when the water table is lower, will lead to higher per-unit extraction costs. Second, the aquifer will be dewatered more quickly than desired by all users as a group because the future availability of water to the individual is uncertain. Third, although it is not likely that a user will pump unless the incremental value of the water in current use exceeds current incremental costs, the uncertainty of future supplies will lead users to ignore the value today of water saved for future use.[4] These effects combine to lead to a faster than optimal depletion of the groundwater stock—and possibly to the destruction of the aquifer.

These external effects (costs borne by individuals other than the decision maker) can be eliminated if all groundwater users merge into a single unit or if regulations are imposed by a central managing body. Using either of these methods simulates the single owner case, wherein any externalities from extraction would be internalized because private and social costs from groundwater use would be combined. But because transaction costs in merging many competing units are so high, support has grown for the alternative approach of centrally managing groundwater basins.

Groundwater is both a stock and a flow resource. The stock portion is the amount of water in the aquifer, and the flow portion refers to the amount that annually recharges the aquifer through percolation from the surface or underground stream flow. Any efficient management plan must take into account both of these characteristics. Neither of the approaches noted above has been successful. As an alternative, we will argue that an institutional framework of well-defined, transferable property rights, which includes a consideration of the unique features of groundwater, is likely to lead to a larger net value from groundwater use than would common access or central management.

THE COMMONALITY PROBLEM

An aquifer is an underground formation of porous, water-bearing rock. Many wells—sometimes thousands—are sunk into the forma-

---

4. The exception would be if rights to future supplies depend on historical rates of pumping.

tion to extract the water. The groundwater supply for most basins is naturally recharged to some extent by water percolating into the aquifer from the surface or from an underground river. Some aquifers receive a large amount of recharge (as a percentage of the stock) while others, such as the Ogallala formation that spreads from northern Nebraska to west Texas, receive very little and can be considered nonrenewable resources.

As long as the total amount of water withdrawn from an aquifer is not greater than the net natural recharge, there is little cause to expect inefficient rates of water withdrawal.[5] Once total extraction exceeds recharge, however, external effects may arise. Groundwater extraction costs increase directly as a result of a drop in the water table. There is a classic divergence between private and social costs. A pumper considers only his own extraction costs in deciding how much to pump; he ignores the increased pumping costs imposed on his fellow groundwater users in that basin.

The quality of water may also be severely affected by extensive overdraft. In many coastal aquifers, for example, saltwater intrusion has become a serious problem. Groundwater naturally flows toward the sea, but excessive pumping can cause the flow to reverse, leading to saline contamination of the aquifer. This problem can be overcome, at a cost, by injecting water into the aquifer to form a barrier against the salt water, but it may take years to flush the salt completely out of the aquifer.

Further, the land may subside when the groundwater pressure level in a confined aquifer is lowered by overpumping, and the water is squeezed out of the clay layers of the aquifer until they compact. If this happens, the overlying land surface drops, and the value of the aquifer diminishes because it can no longer be completely recharged. A land depression of only a few feet can cause surface water distribution systems that operate on gravity to reverse their flow. A decline in the groundwater level may even cause increased seismic fault-

---

5. The one potentially serious problem is the so-called cone of depression that may occur from excessively high pumping over a prolonged period of time. The water table around the well will drop and, depending on the lateral movement of water in the aquifer, recharge may be reduced. The existence of cones of depression thereby affects future pumping costs, the timing of future pumping, or both. As a result, bargaining between adjacent landowners will be necessary to reduce the rate of pumping. This problem will exist under any institutional framework, but under a property rights system individuals will have the incentive to reduce their rate of pumping in general, thereby reducing the severity of any cones of depression.

ing.[6] These are only a few of the physical problems that can result from groundwater overdraft.

While it may not be optimal from an economic perspective to eliminate all of these problems, some of them may be excessive. An optimal solution will be reached only when the marginal benefits and the marginal costs of reducing the externalities are equal. Such a solution is efficient and maximizes the value generated from groundwater use. In addition, it *can* be achieved by individual initiative, provided the institutional structure is designed so that each pumper bears all the costs of and reaps all the benefits from his actions. Unless such steps are taken, the expected increase in groundwater use will only exacerbate current problems.

GROUNDWATER LAW

Groundwater law is legislated by individual states and, therefore, varies considerably in terms of intent and complexity. There are, nevertheless, four basic doctrines of groundwater law in existence today:[7] (1) the English rule of absolute ownership, (2) the American rule of reasonable use, (3) the correlative rights doctrine, and (4) the doctrine of prior appropriation.

The first recorded legal dispute over water arose in England in the 1840s between a mine owner who was dewatering his mine and a nearby tanner whose spring dried up. The court addressed the problem by giving the overlying landowner complete freedom to act without liability. Since the court did not know anything about the hydrologic nature of groundwater, it avoided the issue by classifying groundwater as property in the same way that any rock or mineral on or under an individual's land is classified. This ruling became known as the *English rule of absolute ownership.*

The English rule was adopted in the United States, primarily because of the difficulty in assigning liability when third party effects resulted from groundwater use. As Frank Trelease points out, "It was in the light of this scientific and judicial ignorance that the over-

6. T. L. Holzer, "Faulting Caused by Groundwater Level Declines, San Joaquin, California," *Water Resources Research* 16 (December 1980): 1065–70.

7. F. L. Trelease, "Developments in Groundwater Law," in *Advances in Groundwater Hydrology*, ed. Z. A. Saleem (Minneapolis: American Water Resources Association, 1976), pp. 271–78.

lying owner was given total dominion over his 'property,' that is, a free hand to do as he pleased with water he found within his land, without accountability for damage."[8] The law worked well for a time, mainly because third party injuries were uncommon.

The *American rule of reasonable use* was developed in the United States to soften the extremes of absolute ownership. Under this legal system, overlying landowners have coequal rights to the groundwater, subject to "reasonable" use. These rights are similar to the riparian rights that govern surface water. The determination of reasonableness is primarily a judicial one and is related to the demand of adjacent landowners to the common supply.

A modification of reasonable use is the *correlative rights doctrine*, created by the California courts in 1903. According to this doctrine, all overlying landowners are held to reasonable overlying use, and their rights are considered coequal. In the event that demand for groundwater exceeds supply (e.g., during a drought year), all landowners must decrease their use by the same proportionate amount.

Under the fourth major legal system governing groundwater acquisition, the *doctrine of prior appropriation*, water rights are acquired by use. Use rights are usually granted by permit through application to a public agency (state or local). Rights are often defined as to the quantity of water that may be withdrawn, the uses to which the water may be put, and even the dates when the right may be exercised. Appropriative rights are not limited to overlying use. Furthermore, this right is treated as a "first in time, first in right" system, and preference is given to senior water rights holders. In case of short supply, junior water rights holders may be shut out, as there is no proportionate reduction in use.

In general, the western states follow the appropriation doctrine. California uses the correlative doctrine as well, and the eastern states allocate groundwater according to the reasonableness principle. Most states use a combination of the major doctrines, modified to fit local requirements.

The difference in the application of the law between the East and West can be traced to the higher annual precipitation in the East. Until the recent series of droughts, the East could rely on a surplus of groundwater, and there was little incentive to modify the original legal doctrines of absolute ownership and reasonable use. In the West, however, these doctrines did not work well in the relatively

8. Ibid., p. 272.

arid environment, so correlative and appropriation doctrines were developed. As groundwater overdraft has become a more serious problem in some of the eastern states, it is not surprising that they have started to modify their laws to conform more closely to those in the West.

It is important to note that almost every state declares that water must be put to "beneficial" use. The use of this nebulous term casts a shadow over all water rights, as will become clear as we evaluate groundwater law according to economic criteria, thus enabling us to see to how great an extent groundwater can currently be directed to its most highly valued uses. Such an evaluation is based on three criteria: (1) the extent to which rights are granted with certainty; (2) how effectively third party effects are addressed; and (3) the transferability of the rights.

If the rights to future water are uncertain, there is much less incentive to invest in irrigation equipment and develop water resources. Why undertake a long-term project if there is uncertainty about the availability of one of the most basic raw materials? Uncertain rights to groundwater also affect transferability and the other criteria of third party effects. How can individuals sell rights to something they may not own?

A certainty problem may arise if an aquifer is overappropriated; that is, if there are legal claims to more water than is in an aquifer or an amount far in excess of net natural recharge. If some of these rights are not exercised, there will be no problems. But if these so-called dormant rights are exercised, other users may suddenly find that their own rights are useless. It is not clear whether those with dormant rights will receive their water or whether junior users will have their rights curtailed or eliminated.

Under the appropriation doctrine, however, the issue of dormant rights is clear. If the right is not exercised within a prescribed period of time, it is lost. But under this doctrine, junior rights holders still face uncertainty. In time of short supply, the most junior rights holders may be cut off from any water. The uncertainty of the right is inversely related to the length of time the use right has been held.

The correlative doctrine generates an uncertainty that is spread among all groundwater users. The doctrine does not allocate a certain quantity of water to individual users. Since there is no priority system between correlative users, the quantity available to each user will change as supply changes.

Uncertainty will also exist if the right can be lost by prescription—that is, by court sanction of adverse possession. Finally, the beneficial use doctrine (discussed below) also breeds uncertainty. A use that is considered beneficial today may not be so judged in the future, thereby jeopardizing the right.

By their nature, common pool resources tend to be overutilized if property rights are not clearly defined. Does existing groundwater law satisfy the second criterion for efficient allocation; that is, how well are third party effects accounted for? Several states have found that the total amount of outstanding rights often exceeds the physical capacity of the aquifer. In other words, a physical limit to groundwater pumping has never been set. This is a tricky issue. Some states have confronted the problem by limiting total pumping in previously open access basins to average recharge. This may be a drastic response to the problem, however, as it leads to a significant reduction in the stock value of groundwater. As we will argue below, the optimal solution may be to allow some drawdown of the aquifer.

If a property right is well defined and certain in its tenure, then the right to transfer it will ensure that the resource will be directed to its highest valued uses. The third criterion, the transferability of a water right, therefore, is crucial to the efficient utilization of the resource. Unfortunately, this is where water law fails most miserably, primarily because of the beneficial use doctrine held by most states. Some have interpreted the beneficial use clause to mean that all water use is subject to the condition that it be beneficial to the collective owners of the water; that is, the state or the people. In addition, wasting water is expressly forbidden in many statutes; if a user wastes water, he may lose his right to future water. But what is considered wasteful? This issue is usually determined by a water official or the courts.[9] Furthermore, most states hold that a water right is a usufructuary right in which one has a right to use the water but no physical ownership of it. Water is often owned by the state or by the people of the state.

An intended change in water use may lead to a loss of the right, even if the new use is considered beneficial. The reason is quite simple: If water users want to change either the type or location of use, then they obviously did not need the water for the initially pre-

---

9. With well-defined, transferable private property rights, only an irrational individual will continue to waste water.

scribed use. Originally, they were not really entitled to the water, and the right was lost. Incredible as this may sound, at least a few states act in accordance with this kind of reasoning. For example, the California Constitution has been interpreted as saying that a desire to transfer a water right is equivalent to conceding that the water is not presently being put to beneficial use, and thus an attempt to transfer the right may result in the loss of that right.[10]

Some states have set up controlled groundwater zones in areas with acute water problems (i.e., where there is excess demand).[11] Transfer may be forbidden in these zones. Most states do not allow the transfer of water outside their boundaries, unless there is a reciprocal agreement with the state to which the water is being transferred.

Some states allow transfers within their borders, or at least within a particular groundwater basin, with few restrictions. Others, however, will only allow intra- or interbasin transfers under restricted conditions. For example, California will allow interbasin transfers only if the water is declared to be "surplus."[12] Water is defined to be surplus if it is of no use to any other basin user at a *zero* price. In other words, water can be moved to a more highly valued use only if it is of no value to local users.

In an artificial attempt to allocate water to more highly valued uses, many states have devised a preference system for water use. For example, domestic and municipal uses usually receive top priority, followed by agricultural, industrial, and commercial use. This system will coincide with the true relative values of water only by coincidence and most certainly fails to consider the marginal value of water in the different uses.

Interestingly, one state, Oklahoma, has taken the initiative in assigning transferable rights to groundwater. A 1973 law allows the dewatering of groundwater basins, with the stock allocated on a minimum twenty-year life for the basin.[13] In other words, it will be legal to mine the basin at a rate that will exhaust the supply in no less than twenty years. Water transfers are (presumably) subject only to legal challenges raised by potentially affected third parties.

10. S. Angelides and Eugene Bardach, *Water Banking: How to Stop Wasting Agricultural Water* (San Francisco: Institute for Contemporary Studies, 1978), p. 10.

11. U.S., Department of Energy, "Institutional Constraints on Alternative Water for Energy" (November 1980), p. 32.

12. Angelides and Bardach, *Water Banking*, p. 11.

13. Okla., Stat. Ann. Tit. 82, secs. 1020.1 to 1020.22.

While this is definitely a step toward improving allocative efficiency, the Oklahoma plan appears to be somewhat ill-conceived. The law calls for a hydrologic study to be performed on each basin to determine the amount of water in the aquifer. As of 1981, eight years after the law was enacted, only 6 out of 150 basins in the state had been studied.[14] In addition, treating an aquifer as a nonrenewable resource makes sense only if annual recharge is negligible. Water allocation is still covered by a beneficial use clause, so the state is still in a position to dictate how the water can be used. Oklahoma has taken a step in the right direction, but a better conceived property rights system can be devised.

A system of well-defined, transferable property rights clearly provides economic benefits. The market process provides incentives for using a resource—such as water—in the most efficient manner possible, enabling us to derive the most benefit (measured in dollars) from the fixed quantity of available water. Current groundwater law does not provide either the certainty or the transferability necessary for efficient water use to occur. Further, it does not account for third party effects.

Why, then, have citizens waited so long to make the availability of water a matter of public concern? For decades, problems of excess demand were met by expanding supply networks (aqueducts, canals, and dams) with seemingly little regard for economic or environmental costs.[15] Large water projects in the West were labeled "pork barrel," with special interests and influential constituents as the beneficiaries. The federal government funded water projects with little thought given to whether the projects would pay for themselves. Fortunately, the current political climate is more favorable to evaluating such projects on their net economic merit.

There are two ways to deal with the current problems in groundwater management: (1) change the law to allow for the creation of well-defined, transferable property rights in groundwater; or (2) encourage more governmental management of this precious, common pool resource.

14. Private conversation with Duane A. Smith, hydrologist, Oklahoma Water Resources Board.

15. J.C. DeHaven and J. Hirschleifer, "Feather River Water for Southern California," *Land Economics* 33 (August 1957): 201.

CENTRAL MANAGEMENT OF
GROUNDWATER SUPPLIES

It is apparent that individuals left to act on their own initiative have not used water efficiently. Many analysts have concluded that since the market has failed to allocate this resource efficiently, central management is required. But these analysts have missed a crucial point: The attenuated set of property rights in groundwater does not allow market forces to work effectively.

Central control of groundwater resources already exists to a significant degree. Many states, through the courts and bureaucratic agencies, have the power to decide how and where and how much groundwater will be used. Most states already require that rights holders obtain governmental approval before they transfer their rights to other users and uses. Governmental control is almost total in the so-called controlled groundwater zones. Central management takes other forms as well. The government can assign specific yearly quotas for each individual user, for example. It has also been suggested that pump taxes be enacted to force users to take into account third party effects.

Many criticisms can be directed against the central management of groundwater. One of the commonest is that the management agency would be responsible for determining the value of groundwater among competing users and uses. Such an agency would have to answer a lot of questions regarding the relative values of different uses. Which is a more valuable use of groundwater on the margin: watering livestock or irrigating a wheat field? In the absence of information generated by the market process—namely bid and asked prices—the agency would be in no position to give an accurate or useful response.

The managing body would also have to determine the optimal amount of groundwater that should be held in reserve as insurance against temporary shortfalls in future recharge. (Temporary shortfalls in recharge would lead to higher pumping costs and, if the remaining stock is small, an insufficient supply of groundwater.) The optimal amount would be reached by maintaining the water table at a higher level than if each year's recharge were known with certainty. The decision regarding how much water to set aside depends in part on the user's preference for risk. Keeping a smaller insurance stock means that the user is willing to trade off the possibility of a lower output (due to short supplies or higher costs or both) in some future period against a higher value for present output (since more water is being used in the current period).

For example, an irrigator of an orchard where a very dry year could wipe out a valuable stock of trees is likely to be more risk averse (and thus willing to pay more to stockpile more water) than the producer of a field crop. But since the management agency must act for all basin users collectively, it must assume that all users have the same risk preference. Furthermore, the agency must determine what this average risk preference is—not an easy thing to do. It is likely that the agency would act conservatively, stockpiling a relatively large amount of water and denying users the opportunity to use more water now at the risk of having less water in the future. By adopting such inflexible practices, governmental agencies often adversely influence productivity and profits.

Finally, we must look at the incentives that the management agency would face. The history of governmental management of economic enterprises is not encouraging. There is no a priori reason to assume that groundwater would be managed efficiently, or even that economic efficiency would be one of the agency's real—rather than only stated—objectives. Further, given what we know about such agencies, we would expect the agency to make certain that their largest and most powerful clients (e.g., large farm organizations and municipalities) receive what they demand.

Is there a better way? Is there an institutional arrangement that would give us greater social benefit from the limited water we have? Can property rights be created for a common pool resource such as groundwater?

A PROPERTY RIGHTS ALTERNATIVE

If well-defined, fully transferable property rights were assigned to groundwater, market forces would ensure that the resource is put to its most highly valued uses, thus providing the greatest social benefits from our limited supply. How can we assign such property rights?

Since groundwater is both a stock and a flow resource, a property rights alternative would take these characteristics into account by establishing a two-part right: [16] A perpetual right would be granted

16. B. Wetzel, *Efficient Water Use in California: Economic Modeling of Groundwater Development with Applications to Groundwater Management* (Washington, D.C.: The Rand Corporation, November 1978).

for groundwater's flow component, and each user would receive a fixed percentage of the long-run average annual recharge. The stock component would be allocated as a once-and-for-all property right that could be exercised at any time. The entire groundwater stock, however, might not be allocated. To avoid the many environmental problems that may arise from excessive overdraft, a hydrologic study of the aquifer would be performed to determine how much water could be safely removed from the aquifer before such problems became serious. It is this "safe" amount of "surplus" stock that would be allocated.

The government would still be involved in commissioning or performing the hydrologic study. There is a definite lack of information about groundwater aquifers, and there will always be some uncertainty about how much water they actually contain.[17] This uncertainty can be addressed, however, by periodically updating the hydrologic studies (every five or ten years) and by initially allocating a fixed portion of the so-called temporary surplus. For example, pending the study to be made in five years, 80 percent of the safe surplus would be allocated.

The proposed property rights system would eliminate most of the third party effects associated with uncontrolled groundwater pumping.[18] The fact that pumping costs would increase as the water table is lowered to the long-run safe level poses the most serious remaining problem. We would apparently be left with the incentive to exercise the stock right as soon as possible, thus avoiding higher pumping costs. Given the certainty of the water right and the evidence that there are rapidly diminishing returns to additional water use in any particular period, however, this problem is probably more apparent than real.

Another problem would exist if the aquifer had an irregularly shaped floor. In this case, some users might find that their wells were running dry earlier than others'. This simply means that different users, by virtue of their location over the aquifer, face different extraction costs for the water to which they have rights. The user with rights located over a dry well would have to make arrangements to pump from someone else's well and transfer the water, or else sell his

---

17. Vernon L. Smith, "Water Deeds: A Proposed Solution to the Water Valuation Problem," *Arizona Review* 26 (January 1977): 7–10.
18. S. Yakowitz and L. Duckstein, "Instability in Aquifer Identification: Theory and Case Studies," *Water Resource Research* 16 (December 1980): 1045–64.

water rights. The varying costs of production would be reflected in the price of the water rights.

There are numerous advantages to establishing private property rights in groundwater. Only an ignorant or irrational individual would continue to "waste" water by not directing it to more highly valued uses. Bids by potential water buyers should largely eliminate ignorance in this case. Individual users would be able to allocate their certain share of the supply when and as they see fit, with the incentive to maximize their private and, hence, social benefits from groundwater use. The decision on insurance stocks would be a private one. Those users who are more risk averse would stockpile relatively larger quantities of water than those who have a greater preference for risk. Most important, individuals would reap the benefits from and suffer the costs of their own actions, without imposing any third party effects. It is precisely for this reason that individuals can be given the freedom to act as they wish.

The procedure for actually assigning the rights would be judicial. In terms of economic efficiency, how the rights are initially allocated is irrelevant. The initial allocation, however, would result in potentially large awards of wealth to those who actually gain the water rights. The courts could make this decision based on historical, equitable, or other considerations. But that is not for us to decide here.

CONCLUSION

Recent reports would have us believe that a water shortage might affect the United States in the near future. The problem, however, is not that there is insufficient water, but that with current institutional arrangements the incentives to use it efficiently are tenuous at best. This is especially true with groundwater. Areas of the United States would still experience periodic drought; but under a property rights system, users would have the incentive to seek out the best information available and to plan for such periods. As in all free market activity, those who plan correctly would be rewarded in the marketplace. Those who use available information and correctly predict the pattern of future recharge would have a relatively larger long-run supply of water available than those who do not.

A change in the rules of the game played by groundwater users can ensure that this resource will be used wisely. This can be accomplished without continuous intervention by any governmental, bureaucratic body. A wise change would promote individual freedom of action for all groundwater users. Each individual would be able to decide how, when, and where to use his available supply, with every incentive to move the resource to its highest valued use. Society would also benefit as groundwater would be efficiently and effectively managed and its maximum value realized. Assigning well-defined, transferable property rights to groundwater would enable individual users who do well for themselves also to do good for society.

Chapter 7

REGULATION, INCENTIVES, AND POLLUTION*

For many individuals, all other natural resource problems pale when compared with a continued pollution of our environment. Despoliation of air and water is compelling evidence to some that, in the relentless pursuit of material wealth and well-being, our environment has been intentionally and maliciously mistreated. It is still difficult, for example, to erase the mental image of the Cuyahoga River in Ohio—so polluted by industrial waste that it caught fire.

Many people believe that pollution problems are a natural result of our capitalist system, with its emphasis on profits instead of people, and of our pursuit of higher technology. Even though it is convenient to blame capitalism and the pursuit of sophisticated technology for pollution and diseased wildlife, neither of these so-called culprits can be held truly responsible. Pollution problems also exist in countries with planned (that is, nonmarket) economies.[1] Even more to the point, technology is neutral and will respond to whatever signals (economic incentives) are given in the economy.[2] If nat-

*This chapter was written by David T. Fractor, Research Associate at the Center for Political Economy and Natural Resources.

1. William J. Baumol and Wallace E. Oates, *Economics, Environmental Policy, and the Quality of Life* (Englewood Cliffs, N. J.: Prentice-Hall, 1979), chap. 5.

2. Lloyd D. Orr, "Social Costs, Incentive Structures, and Environmental Policies," in *Bureaucracy vs. Environment*, ed. John Baden and Richard L. Stroup (Ann Arbor: University of Michigan Press, 1981), p. 50.

ural resources are being overexploited, it is because improper signals are directing users away from conservation.

POLLUTION: A CASE OF MARKET FAILURE

In an economy with well-defined and transferable property rights, individuals and firms have every incentive to use resources as efficiently as possible. Furthermore, they will take into account the opportunity costs of their actions; that is, the highest valued alternative use of a human, technological, or environmental resource.

For example, if the owner of a factory also owns an adjacent stream that is good for fishing, he can charge fishermen for access to that stream. If the factory dumps pollutants into the stream, reducing the value of fishing, revenues from the fishermen will decrease. Therefore, the owner will rationally consider reducing the amount of pollutants his factory emits into the stream. The socially efficient solution would be to reduce pollution until the marginal cost of pollution control equals the marginal revenue from selling fishing permits. Under such an arrangement, the owner would benefit from the additional revenue and fishermen would benefit by having a pleasant place to practice their sport.

Alternatively, what if another individual has clear, easily defended rights to the stream? Just as factory owners cannot dump garbage on someone else's car, they could not dump waste in someone else's water. They must respect the rights of others or risk being taken to court.

But what if no one owns the adjacent stream? Suppose the stream is considered common property. Under these conditions, factory owners can no longer receive revenue from the sale of fishing rights. Nor would they fear prosecution in court. For factory owners, then, the opportunity cost of the stream is essentially zero, and they have no incentive to reduce pollution of the stream. As a result, everyone bears the cost.

This helps explain why pollution can be a problem in a market-oriented economy. The lack of property rights in certain resources can result in economic agents ignoring the true opportunity costs of their actions. It follows directly that air and common water resources will be overpolluted. It also follows that nonmarket-oriented economies, with even fewer direct incentives, will have pollution problems as well.

Pollution is the residual or byproduct of a production process — the smoke from a factory, the sewage from a chemical company, or the exhaust from an automobile. When air and water are common pool resources, it is easy to ignore the social costs of pollution. When calculating the cost of owning an automobile, for example, we usually consider gas, oil, depreciation, insurance, and the like. But an automobile's exhaust emissions contain noxious substances that pollute the air, and, in an area like Los Angeles, driving contributes to often toxic air conditions. Smog can cause respiratory problems and burning eyes and can eventually kill some forms of plant life. In the Lake Arrowhead area, for example, just sixty miles east of Los Angeles, pine trees are dying from the city's smog. We can conclude, then, that spewing poison into the air we breathe represents one cost of driving. The major cause of this health hazard is not the unfeeling, unthinking automobile owner, but the common property aspects attached to the air itself. No one owns the air and, therefore, everyone is at liberty to misuse it without bearing any personal cost.

Society would be better off if all individuals were made responsible for the damages they inflict on the environment. But how can this best be accomplished? A socially efficient solution demands that pollution emissions for any activity be reduced until the marginal damage (measured in dollars) from one additional unit of pollutant equals the marginal cost of reducing pollution by one unit. If the law required that pollution be at a level where marginal pollution control costs exceed marginal damages, then society would lose because a more desired activity is being restricted too much. For instance, if eliminating one unit of pollution reduces pollution damages by ten dollars but the cost of controlling that unit is fifteen dollars, then pollution has been reduced too much.

Aside from extending property rights to air and water resources, two methods can be used to control pollution: (1) Price it by imposing a tax based on the amount of pollution emitted, or (2) require a fixed reduction in the amount of pollution produced.[3] For both efficiency and equity reasons, most economists favor the tax method, more commonly known as effluent fees. Nevertheless, most pollution control legislation calls for a uniform reduction in pollution emissions. Yet direct pollution regulation is not only inefficient, it

---

3. See Baumol and Oates, *Economics*; Edwin S. Mills, *The Economics of Environmental Quality* (New York: W. W. Norton, 1978); and Frederick R. Anderson et al., *Environmental Improvement Through Economic Incentives* (Baltimore: Johns Hopkins University Press, 1977).

also stifles innovation by requiring specific pollution control devices or techniques and by implicitly encouraging firms to ignore the regulations by providing insufficient monitoring and enforcement.

Consider two plants in the same area that emit the same amount of SO_2 (sulfur dioxide), causing damages estimated at ten dollars per unit of pollutant. Legislation is enacted that requires a 50 percent reduction in pollution emission for each plant. The marginal cost of reducing pollution for the first plant is six dollars and fourteen for the second plant. The difference in pollution control costs may be due to the kinds of products produced, the quantity produced, or the production techniques used in each plant.

Does legislation lead to an efficient resolution of the problem? Clearly not. For the first plant, the reduction in pollution damages exceeds marginal control costs (ten dollars is greater than six dollars), and the reverse is true for the second plant. If, instead, an effluent fee equal to pollution damages is charged, different results would ensue. At a fee of ten dollars per unit of pollution, each plant would reduce pollution until the marginal costs of pollution control equaled the effluent fee. The first plant might reduce pollution by 75 percent and the second plant by 45 percent. Pollution would thus be reduced by an average of 60 percent, and total marginal costs for both plants (twenty dollars) at equilibrium would be the same as under direct regulation. In other words, there would be 10 percent less pollution with no increase in costs at the margin.

Perhaps this seems too simple an answer to a complicated problem. Is there a catch here? Not at all. Under an effluent fee program, firms will adjust until incremental damages and control costs are equal. With a uniform reduction requirement, on the other hand, firms are simply forced to curtail pollution. Because firms are not allowed to adjust to their most efficient level of pollution control, the required reduction may be very costly for some firms and relatively inexpensive for others.

The case is often made that direct regulation is more equitable than effluent fees because an equiproportionate reduction in pollution is required for all firms.[4] But unless all firms are identical, there will be a disparity in pollution control costs. With effluent fees, on the other hand, all polluters pay the same for the use of the re-

---

4. Baumol and Oates, *Economics*, p. 235, and Anderson et al., *Environmental Improvement*, p. 151.

source—that is, the air or water. Because of this, many economists contend that effluent fees are the most equitable method for controlling pollution.

Some people fear that effluent fees give some firms a license to pollute, since the amount of pollution is not explicitly limited. This is indeed true. The amount paid for this license depends on the amount of pollution emitted by each firm. A system of effluent fees would enable firms to reduce their effluent payments by reducing emissions. They would in fact do so as long as the incremental cost of reducing pollution were less than the per unit effluent charge. By pricing what is otherwise an unpriced factor in the production process, effluent fees would lead to a reduction in pollution and an increase in air and water quality.

When considering institutional change to correct a defect in the market, we must determine whether the increase in efficiency justifies the cost of the new program. Pollution control programs must be assessed in the same way. To administer a system of either effluent charges or direct regulation effectively, we must be able to monitor discharge points and accurately assess pollution damages. Direct regulation, however, also requires knowledge of pollution control costs for all dischargers and for all pollution control technology, a virtually insurmountable and extremely costly information requirement. We can conclude, then, that the information required for control by effluent fees will always be less than for direct regulation.

Given that a system of effluent fees is the most efficient way to handle damage caused by pollution, it may seem odd that some businesses favor direct controls. For insights into this seeming inconsistency and for other responses to approaches in pollution control, we turn to an examination of federal legislation.

POLLUTION CONTROL LEGISLATION

Until the mid-1950s, responsibility for pollution control lay primarily with state and local governments.[5] As the nation became more concerned with environmental matters, however, federal involvement in pollution control was inevitable. Decentralized control, for ob-

5. This section is drawn primarily from Baumol and Oates, *Economics*, chap. 21, and Mills, *Environmental Quality*, chap. 7.

vious reasons, gave states little incentive to abate pollution that crossed their boundaries. Prior to 1970, federal programs were administered by a number of agencies, primarily the Department of Interior and the Department of Health, Education, and Welfare. Then in 1970, the Environmental Protection Agency (EPA) was created to administer all important federal environmental programs.

The first comprehensive legislative act concerning water pollution was the federal Water Pollution Control Act of 1956. The act made federal grants available to local governments for constructing sewage treatment plants. In addition, the federal government was given the authority to study water quality in interstate water bodies. If it was found that pollution was hazardous to human health, a federal-state conference could be convened. Although the authority has rarely been exercised, the act also permits the federal government to file suit in federal court to force dischargers to take required actions.

The Water Pollution Control Act was amended in 1965 to establish ambient quality standards on interstate waterways. These standards were established in an attempt to ease the circumstances under which the courts could be used to force polluters to take action. It was reasoned that water quality falling below the standards was prima facie evidence that the dischargers were violating the law. Enforcement remained elusive, however, because the government had to prove that violation of a standard was caused by a particular discharger.

The act was amended in 1972 over President Nixon's veto. Under the Water Pollution Act Amendments, the EPA was charged with establishing a permit system for pollution discharge. After all permits have been issued, it will be illegal to discharge wastes from a point source without a permit. As Lloyd Orr points out, "The basis for discharge permits is that 'best practicable technology' (BPT) be installed by July 1, 1977, and that 'best available technology' (BAT) be installed by July 1, 1983. The average of an industry group provides the basis for BPT. The best performance in an industry provides the basis for 'economically achievable' BAT."[6] Congress set a goal of eliminating *all* discharges by 1985.

The EPA's task is a burdensome one. By 1976, nearly sixty-three thousand industrial and municipal dischargers had been identified. To determine "economically achievable" abatement technology, the

6. Orr, "Social Costs," p. 52.

EPA must be aware of available production and waste treatment technologies for *each* discharger. In addition, their progress has been impeded by their involvement in many lengthy court challenges of the proposed standards.

Edwin S. Mills has nicely summarized the evolution and current state of federal water pollution control:

> National policy in this area has been characterized by increasing boldness and stridency, if not wisdom, since 1956. . . . In principle, almost nothing an industrial firm does is outside the purview of EPA. Its activities are limited mainly by the budget Congress provides. Major industrial decisions were formerly made on the basis of competitive and profitability considerations; they are now made jointly with government lawyers and technicians.[7]

The passage of air pollution legislation and management has followed a similar path. The Clean Air Act of 1963 gave the federal government its first enforcement powers in the abatement of air pollution. Similar to the Water Pollution Control Act of 1956, the Clean Air Act authorized the study of areas where health problems are potentially caused by air pollution. The regulatory power of the act applied only to stationary sources. The Motor Vehicle Air Pollution Act of 1965, however, authorized the first auto emission standards, beginning with 1968 models. Modest reduction levels in carbon monoxide (CO) and hydrocarbon (HC) discharges were set. For 1970 models, the standards were much stricter, as emissions of CO and HC were cut to one-half the preregulatory levels.

The Air Quality Act of 1967 designated a set of air quality regions and asked the appropriate states to establish ambient air quality standards for these regions. If these standards were deemed unsatisfactory, the federal government could then establish its own standards.

The major piece of air pollution legislation, the 1970 Clean Air Amendments, gave the EPA the responsibility for setting air quality standards. The EPA set the primary standards, below which human health was threatened, and gave the states only a short time to implement them. For stationary sources, the EPA undertook the same detailed approach as it did for water pollution. It also required reductions of pollution emissions from new cars, beginning in 1975, that were 5 percent of pre-1967 emission levels for CO and HC. In addi-

---

7. Mills, *Environmental Quality*, pp. 184, 187.

tion, the EPA established standards for nitrogen oxides (NO_x). The 1970 act is unique in that it stated what the ambient standards were, rather than establishing guidelines for the EPA to use in setting its own standards.

Pollution can be seen in two very different ways. When viewed as an abnormal occurrence, regulation takes an all-or-nothing attitude toward pollution control. If a firm exceeds the established pollution limits, it is subject to criminal sanctions and the police powers of the state. On the other hand, pollution can be seen as a normal consequence of activities whose costs are incorrectly reflected in market prices. In this view, the problem can be alleviated by establishing corrective prices, or effluent fees. By and large, government has adopted the first position.

Enforcing complex pollution standards requires an enormous amount of time and information and a much larger bureaucracy than if effluent fees were the primary regulatory instrument. But bureaucratic efficiency is not one of the EPA's concerns, and it continues to oppose the use of effluent fees.[8] There is some evidence that many employees of the EPA fear that the agency will be dissolved or that substituting effluent fees for direct regulation might reduce the discretionary power that the EPA now enjoys.

The current regulatory environment actually encourages stagnation in pollution control. An industry that develops a new technique for reducing harmful discharges may be unwilling to use it because it may lead to a tightening of emission standards for the entire industry. For example, the EPA discovered that cement plants were capable of filtering out significant levels of harmful particulate emissions. As a result, the agency imposed emission levels for cement plants that were more stringent than emission levels for electric power plants. In other words, electric power plants were allowed to pollute more. Angered by the supposed inequities sanctioned by the EPA, a Portland cement plant challenged the agency's rate structure in court. In denying the challenge, the court argued that if an industry can more effectively control emissions, it should be required to do so.[9] Because of such cases, many critics accuse the EPA of penalizing innovation, leading to continued rather than reduced pollution levels.

The same perverse incentive applies to firms within an industry. If a firm has many plants and develops a new pollution control tech-

8. Ibid., p. 218.
9. Baumol and Oates, *Economics*, pp. 339–40.

nology for one of them, it may become the standard that must be met as the "best available technology" for all of the firm's plants. Under the present institutional structure, the costs of doing research and development on pollution control devices are often prohibitive. Regulatory agencies depend on negative reinforcement to effect industry compliance to pollution standards, but such perverse incentives lead to discontent and stagnation.

As previously noted, the 1956 Water Pollution Control Act made federal grants available to local governments for sewage treatment plants, but only capital expenditures were to be subsidized. This limitation biases the pollution control effort by creating a disincentive against controls that might reduce the quantity of effluent, favoring instead "end of pipe" treatment.[10] While municipalities build more elaborate treatment facilities, maintenance budgets suffer, and existing facilities fall into disrepair.

The costs of complying with direct pollution control are very high. It is estimated that required pollution control expenditures will reach nearly one-half trillion dollars for the 1980s.[11] Yet, business tends to favor direct control.[12] Why? There are three possible reasons. First, effluent fees, once enacted, are not easily avoided. Second, under direct controls, firms can attempt to avoid compliance by negotiating with regulators or by charging inequities in the courts. Many corporations have successfully delayed complying with pollution control standards for up to ten years by challenging the regulations in court. Third, direct control could limit the entry of new firms into polluting industries, thereby increasing the profits of existing firms.

We must not ignore the political motivations involved in the pollution control process. Congressional legislation creates agencies that hold sweeping power, providing concrete evidence that "action" is being taken against pollution. Compare the political palatability of direct control with effluent fees that, after all, are merely licenses to pollute. Yet, even potential special interest supporters of the EPA believe that direct control is not the best way to proceed. In fact, effluent charges are now favored by the National Audubon Society,

10. Orr, "Social Costs," p. 54.
11. Baumol and Oates, *Economics*, p. 341.
12. Ibid., pp. 241–42.

the Sierra Club, and other environmental organizations.[13] Two cases, one on water and one on air, illustrate the potential for effluent fees and the political nature of pollution control legislation.

EFFLUENT CHARGES ON THE DELAWARE ESTUARY

The Delaware estuary is an eighty-six-mile reach of the Delaware River that stretches from Trenton, New Jersey, to Liston Point, Delaware—one of the most highly industrialized and densely populated regions in the world. Residual waste from municipal treatment plants and industrial discharge have placed very heavy oxygen demands on the estuary. Oxygen is used to break down the organic matter, and as the dissolved oxygen (DO) content of the estuary decreases, fewer species of fish can survive. If the DO is exhausted, the organic residuals are broken down anaerobically, resulting in the foul odors found in some bodies of water.

A 1966 study conducted by the federal Water Pollution Control Administration attempted to assess external pollution costs as well as control costs associated with four alternative policies: (1) least cost (LC); (2) uniform treatment (UT); (3) single effluent charge (SECh); and (4) zone effluent charge (ZECh).[14]

The first alternative, the least-cost (LC) solution, was theoretically the cheapest solution that could be achieved. LC is found by using a detailed mathematical program and requires precise information on waste treatment costs of all discharge points and direct controls on all waste discharges. Treatment would be concentrated at points along the estuary where oxygen levels could be increased most inexpensively. Because information requirements are far greater than any regulatory agency could reasonably acquire, the least-cost solution is useful primarily as a benchmark against which the alternatives can be compared.

The second alternative was the uniform treatment (UT) solution in which each discharger would be required to reduce waste discharge by the same percentage. This form of direct control is the easiest to

13. Anderson et al., *Environmental Improvement*, p. 150, and Mills, *Environmental Quality*, p. 218.

14. Allen V. Kneese, *Economics and the Environment* (New York: Penguin, 1977), chap. 7.

Table 7-1. Pollution Treatment Cost under Alternative Programs
(in millions of dollars per year).

DO Standard (PPM)	Program			
	LC	*VT*	*SECh*	*ZECh*
2	1.6	5.0	2.4	2.4
3–4	7.0	20.0	12.0	8.6

Source: Allen V. Kneese, *Economics and the Environment* (New York: Penguin, 1977), p. 164.

administer but the most expensive to implement, for it ignores the fact that control costs vary across polluters.

The third and fourth alternatives were effluent charges. The single effluent charge (SECh) solution imposes the same per unit fee for waste discharge at all points along the estuary. The zone effluent charge (ZECh) solution divides the estuary into zones and levies a uniform effluent charge in each zone.

The estimated costs for achieving two DO standards are given in Table 7-1. The DO standard of three to four parts per million (ppm) was considered the most economically justifiable when benefits of pollution reduction were taken into account. As expected, the UT solution was by far the most expensive. In current dollars, the ZECh solution saves about $150 million over the UT solution, because pollution control is concentrated where control costs are lower. As for considerations of equity, only the effluent charges distribute costs equally (per zone or for the entire estuary) among all waste dischargers. For the Delaware estuary, the potential for effluent fees as a lower cost alternative for pollution control has been clearly demonstrated.

CLEAN COAL/DIRTY AIR

Many think that pollution control legislation, no matter how inefficient, will at least lead to a cleaner environment. As we shall see, however, this is not always the case.[15]

15. Robert W. Crandall, "Ackerman and Hassler's Clean Coal/Dirty Air," *Bell Journal of Economics* 12 (Autumn 1981): 677–82.

Section 111 of the Clean Air Act Amendments of 1977 was aimed at reducing sulfur dioxide emissions. To this end, it requires stack-gas scrubbers for all new coal-fired plants. Stack-gas scrubbers work by "scrubbing" the gas that is produced when coal is burned, removing sulfur dioxide (SO_2) in the process. Rather than set emission standards for these plants, the EPA requires plants to install the "best available technology" for pollution control, and in this case the best available technology is stack-gas scrubbers. This policy, however, was directed toward forcing use of a particular technology rather than reducing pollution. The burning of low sulfur coal is not permitted without the scrubbers, even if it emits less sulfur oxide than high sulfur coal. This is apparently irrational. In addition, the scrubbers are effective only if operated according to specifications; otherwise, they hardly reduce sulfur emissions. Given the EPA's inability to monitor most plants, there is little incentive to operate the scrubbers efficiently. In sum, requiring the use of a given technology rather than adherence to established air quality standards is both costly and environmentally destructive. Neither efficiency nor environmental quality is served by it. Why, then, does this policy exist?

There is evidence that the passage of Section 111 was based entirely on political considerations. Western coal is low in sulfur, while much of the coal found in the Midwest and Appalachia is high in sulfur. A policy of uniform emission standards would probably lead to a substitution of low sulfur coal for high sulfur coal. Requiring stack-gas scrubbers for all new plants, regardless of the sulfur content of the coal used, eliminates the incentive of eastern and midwestern users to switch to western coal.

It is not mere coincidence that the chairmen of both authorizing committees for the EPA when the legislation was passed were from West Virginia, one of the leading eastern (high sulfur) coal-producing states. So was the Senate majority leader. The White House and Congress were also aware that only eastern coal workers were affiliated with the United Mine Workers.

The Clean Coal/Dirty Air case illustrates an important economic point. We must look beyond stated intentions and objectives and focus on the secondary, unstated, and sometimes unintended implications of policy actions. It is clear that the purpose of this legislative approach was not to reduce pollution, but to implicitly subsidize politically powerful special interests.

A VEHICLE POLLUTION TAX

A system of effluent fees constitutes a less costly alternative to direct regulation for achieving desired levels of pollution control. Most of our analysis, however, has focused on stationary pollution sources, such as sewage systems and smokestacks. For certain areas of the country, such as the Los Angeles Basin, the major source of pollution is nonstationary; that is, pollution from motor vehicles. Can effluent fees be assigned to motor vehicles without leading us into an administrative nightmare? Edwin Mills has proposed that vehicle pollution can indeed be taxed, providing at least a beginning in designing innovative, efficient institutions for controlling nonstationary pollution.[16]

Under Mills's plan, damages would be calculated for different pollutants emitted by motor vehicles. The tax would be based on the amount of each pollutant that is produced per mile of driving. The pollution taxes could be calculated and collected during annual vehicle registration by multiplying the charge per unit of pollutants per mile by the number of miles driven. Since pollution emission levels for motor vehicles change over time, the car would be retested for emission levels at the time of registration and charges recalculated accordingly.

Automobile manufacturers would no longer be required to meet emission standards before selling their cars. Nevertheless, competitive pressures would encourage them to innovate and produce cars that pollute less. No one would be prohibited from driving a car that pollutes heavily, although the high pollution taxes would tend to discourage such behavior. Most important, drivers would finally be confronted with the true social costs of their actions. The cost of pollution control is high, but it is now disguised in the total cost of a new automobile.

Modifications to the tax program have been proposed. For example, the tax per unit of pollutant could vary depending on the region. Regions with dirtier air would charge a higher tax than would regions with cleaner air. Also, since older cars are heavier polluters and tend to be owned by lower income individuals, there might be equity—if not efficiency—reasons to levy a lower tax on used cars.

16. Mills, *Environmental Quality*, pp. 233–39.

It might seem suicidal for a politician to propose a pollution tax on motor vehicles. But such a plan could significantly benefit the public, industry, and government. The price of new automobiles would probably decline since they would no longer be forced to include expensive pollution control equipment. Air pollution from automobiles would be substantially reduced. Best of all, the true costs of abatement would be realized and paid for by those who produce the pollution.

CONCLUSION

Has increased federal intervention in pollution control been successful? Results are mixed.[17] Sulfur dioxide levels have been dramatically reduced in major U.S. cities, but the concentration of suspended particulates in many areas still exceeds federal standards. While carbon monoxide levels from automobile emissions have been reduced, emissions of hydrocarbons and nitrogen oxides continue to increase. In some waterways, fish have reappeared and DO content has increased, but concentrations of pesticides and heavy metals are often above recommended levels.

Have the improvements, where they exist, justified their cost? It is safe to say that the environment could have been improved more for the same amount of expenditures. Proper incentive mechanisms, such as effluent fees, would encourage innovation in pollution control and reduce environmentally damaging emissions to socially optimal amounts. No control mechanism is perfect or costless to implement, but when environmental damage warrants controls on the quantity of polluting residuals produced, we should seek controls that restrict pollution as long as marginal external pollution damages exceed marginal control costs.

Where excessive pollution exists, it is because air and water are treated as free goods and, as such, do not enter a firm's or an individual's cost calculations. Taking into account the value of these resources in alternative uses would enable us to achieve the proper balance between environmental quality and all other things we value.

---

17. Baumol and Oates, *Economics*, chap. 21.

Chapter 8

THE DEMISE OF THE SAGEBRUSH REBELLION AND OTHER VANQUISHED DREAMS

Institutions structure information and incentives, and individuals, whether public servants or private citizens, are consistently sensitive to how decisions affect their self-interest. In terms of net social welfare, the information and incentives faced by decision makers in public land management agencies commonly yield flawed management actions.[1] This has happened because bureaucratic entrepreneurs have been allowed to tap the common pool of federal resource wealth and the federal treasury in order to exercise their individual visions and plans for bureaucratic expansion. Yet the belief persists that when "right-thinking" people gain decision-making power through the elective process, movements like the Sagebrush Rebellion become redundant and unnecessary.

As its main goal, the Sagebrush Rebellion has fought for the transfer of federal lands to the states. Unfortunately, neither the problems articulated by the rebels nor the proposed solutions have been properly specified. A transition from one public bureaucracy to another will neither address nor solve the basic problems. It will merely shift the locus of conflict and possibly rearrange the sets of winners and losers. Regardless of who holds the political reins of power, the prob-

---

1. For a further discussion of federal controls of western rangeland, see the Pacific Institute volume by Gary D. Libecap entitled *Locking Up the Range: Federal Land Controls and Grazing* (Cambridge, Mass.: Ballinger, 1981).

lems inherent in bureaucratic management will persist and eventually give rise to future rebellions.

To ask if one supports the Sagebrush Rebellion is roughly analogous to asking if one supports changes in the American health care system. The answer, of course, depends on the consequences of the changes advocated. In supporting reforms of the health care system, one would not necessarily advocate voodoo health care, faith healing, snake handling, or socialized medicine.

In much the same way, one must consider the likely outcomes of the changes advocated by the Sagebrush rebels. While the reforms most commonly advanced by supporters of the rebellion will not guarantee increased efficiency, improved environmental quality, or equity, other reforms are decidedly promising—especially those that are feared the most. A coalition of environmentalists, fiscal conservatives, and individuals who value freedom may arise to address these issues, converting the Sagebrush Rebellion into a Sagebrush Reformation, grounded in empirical data and theories of modern political economy.

It has been said that with Ronald Reagan in the White House and James Watt in the Department of Interior the Sagebrush Rebellion should disband because it is no longer needed to lobby for change. However, those who support such a course are seriously mistaken.

Some members and supporters of the Reagan administration have confidently claimed that the conditions prompting the Sagebrush Rebellion were generated by a lot of "bad people." Now that the good guys are in charge, we are told, the problems will soon be resolved or at least substantially ameliorated. This attitude provides a dangerous example of political naïveté and economic ignorance. The problems cannot be solved until institutions force decision makers to face the true benefits and opportunity costs of alternative actions and the comparative values of alternative mixes of joint products. There must also be incentives to act on this information.

CONSTITUENCY OF THE
SAGEBRUSH REBELLION

Although American citizens have been blessed with an especially benign political environment, even they are beginning to understand that government is the most efficient engine ever developed for the generation of plunder. But when the government provides a context of law and order and an institutional infrastructure that enables individuals to concentrate on cooperative and productive activities rather than on offensive and defensive transfer activities, the net social product can be dramatically enhanced. Fortunately, there are entrepreneurs in the private sector who benefit society—and themselves—by systematically moving resources to more highly valued uses, providing a source of growth, prosperity, and increased social welfare.

The United States Constitution has given us the best recipe ever written for improving social welfare. Over the past century, however, beginning with *Munn* v. *Illinois* in 1877, *political* entrepreneurs have moved us from a society where "getting ahead" required productivity to a different one in which some of the best investments lie in simply transferring wealth from one group (without their willing consent) to another, or in defending oneself against such attempts. The governmental apparatus is used freely to support this transfer society.[2] When the government allocates resources, the payoff comes from investments made to change the rules of the political game and to defend against such changes. The Sagebrush Rebellion is best understood in this context.

The supporters of the Sagebrush Rebellion believe that their share of the allocations would be enhanced if the management and control of federal lands were shifted to the states. They are probably correct. Bureaucrats in the state capital are likely to be more accessible and responsive to local interests and lobbyists than those who operate out of the labyrinth of BLM offices, locally, regionally, or in Washington. Depending on the probabilities of success, investments made in promoting the Sagebrush Rebellion may have been rational in terms of first order consequences and almost surely in terms of second order consequences. When decisions are made in the political arena, however, protracted and vitriolic conflict can be expected.

The active supporters of the Sagebrush Rebellion have been predominantly cattlemen and sheepmen, oil and other energy operators, miners, and representatives of other commodity groups. Representatives of the forest products industry have been notably absent from the rebellion's ranks, however, perhaps because of the peculiarities of federal timber management and the implicit subsidies currently made available to these firms.

---

2. Terry Anderson and Peter J. Hill, *The Birth of a Transfer Society* (Stanford, Calif.: Hoover Institution Press, 1980).

The decided lack of environmentalist support for the rebellion is initially quite puzzling. It is, after all, obvious that despite reasonable intentions, bureaucratic entrepreneurs in the Forest Service, the BLM, the Bureau of Reclamation, the Army Corps of Engineers, and the Bureau of Indian Affairs have consistently and systematically subsidized the deterioration of environmental quality. Examples of such abuse are legion.

The Forest Service, controlling 187 million acres of public land, was established in 1905 to bring scientific, businesslike management to U.S. forests. It has employed science, but it has shown little regard for economy or efficiency as it has gone about controlling vast tracts of forest and wilderness land. It has terraced vast portions of our national forests, planned recreational developments in wilderness areas, and arranged extensive deficit timber sales. In general, the Forest Service has roaded and logged forests that are de facto wilderness areas, using methods that would fail the cost-versus-revenue calculations of Weyerhauser or Boise Cascade.[3]

The other land management agencies have records that are no less discouraging. The BLM has chained and has scheduled for chaining millions of acres of pinyon-juniper ecosystems in the "Elfin Forests" of the Southwest.[4] It has also designed extraordinarily controversial rest-rotation programs for use on 87 percent of their grazing areas.[5] The Bureau of Reclamation has destroyed winter range by building the Teton Dam and other projects that can be justified only at interest rates no greater than about 4 percent, while ignoring the negative externalities imposed by their projects.[6] The Bureau of Indian Affairs has outlawed traditional checks on overgrazing and has fostered the development of the worst range conditions in the United States, impoverishing Indians in the name of communal ownership.[7]

3. See Barney Dowdle, "An Institutional Dinosaur with an Ace: Or, How to Piddle Away Public Timber Wealth and Foul the Environment in the Process," in *Bureaucracy vs. Environment*, ed. John Baden and Richard Stroup (Ann Arbor: University of Michigan Press, 1981), pp. 170–85; and Marion Clawson, "The National Forests," *Science* 191 (1976): 762–67.

4. See Ronald M. Lanner, "Chained to the Bottom," in *Bureaucracy vs. Environment*, pp. 154–69.

5. See Sabine Kremp, "A Perspective on BLM Grazing Policy," in *Bureaucracy vs. Environment*, pp. 124–53.

6. See Bernard Shanks, "Dams and Disasters: The Social Problems of Water Development Policies," in *Bureaucracy vs. Environment*, pp. 108–23.

7. See Gary D. Libecap and Ronald N. Johnson, "The Navajo and Too Many Sheep," in *Bureaucracy vs. Environment*, pp. 87–107.

At the same time, the Army Corps of Engineers has attempted to justify the expansion of its activities by referring to an energy crisis that was generated primarily by governmental policies.[8]

Environmentalists, fiscal conservatives, and those who value liberty agree that the current system consistently displays poor judgment when these programs are supported. Yet, to date, the Sagebrush Rebellion has failed to unite these groups. A failure to understand and conceptualize the true source of the problem has caused many to label the Sagebrush Rebellion the "Sagebrush Ripoff." The charge is not without merit.

Although marginal improvement could possibly be made by transferring federal lands to the states, there are few a priori reasons to expect any significant improvements simply because control is transferred from one bureaucracy to another. In terms of environmental quality, equity, efficiency, and enhanced cooperation, a workable solution to the problem lies in a reliance on private property rights and the rule of willing consent. Only when land users face the true costs and benefits of their actions will productivity and environmental concern prevail. And only then can individuals be allowed to do as they wish. In other words, accountability is a prerequisite for productive behavior, for environmental sensitivity, and for individual freedom.

In the private sector, the asset value of the land is the voice of the future. It holds the owner's wealth hostage to good management. Any erosion of productive land, any scarring of scenic land, or any destruction of habitat valued by scientists or clubs (for example, the Audubon Society and the Nature Conservancy) will harm *society* over the long run. More important, such irresponsible behavior reduces the owner's wealth as well by lowering the land's asset value. Land values—that is, the present capitalized value of *all* future services from the land—hold the owner accountable.

Environmentalists are sensitive to the problems caused by governmental management of the land. But they, too, confidently attribute the causes of the problems to "bad" administration by "bad" people. Even so, they still believe that their interests will be best served by retaining the land in federal ownership. Their arguments are couched in terms of the public interest, general social welfare, and the threat to flora and fauna. Obviously, however, members of envi-

8. See Shanks, "Dams and Disasters."

ronmental interest groups have no monopoly on virtue. They also attempt to use the political process to transfer the control of resources to themselves. Even though we may all share many of their tastes and preferences, many of us strongly contest their response to the problem. Again, the efficient, equitable, and environmentally sensitive solution to the land management issue centers on private property rights and the rule of willing exchange.

THE FUNDAMENTAL ECONOMIC
PROBLEMS OF SOCIETY

Resources have been scarce since the Garden of Eden. Some things of value—that is, some combination of time, effort, and money—must be expended to obtain scarce resources. Such things have an economic value. Thus, asserting that something has an economic value merely suggests that people are willing to trade off other things of value to obtain it. Economic values include more than goods that carry a price tag.

Since resources are scarce in all societies, the first problem of social organization is how to use the available mix of resources to yield the highest assortment of ends. As Friedrich A. Hayek states, "It is rather a problem of how to secure the best use of resources known to any of the members of society, for ends whose relative importance only these individuals know."[9]

We can see that the fundamental problem of forest management is one of planning. To produce the social optimum, the planners must know (1) how badly people want extra units of each product, (2) how to produce each product most efficiently in each specific location, and (3) how to motivate people to produce each product efficiently. Unless answers to these questions are known and implemented, optimal production will occur only by accident, and it is probably safe to assume that such accidents are exceedingly rare.

How can answers to these questions best be generated in a constantly changing environment? Both preferences and opportunities are in continual flux. Because it is exceedingly difficult for a large bureaucracy to be time and place specific, we can begin to appreciate the problems that even the most competent public land managers must confront.

9. Friedrich A. Hayek, *Individualism and Economic Order* (Chicago: Henry Regnery, 1972), p. 78.

Some form of decentralization is required if production is to be optimized. The Forest Service is divided into 9 regions and subdivided into 178 national forests; each forest is further divided into ranger districts. But this arrangement is not good enough. To be responsive to changing demands and opportunities (e.g., the demand for a specific type of lumber is down while that for hiking trails is up), the decision maker must know the relative changes in preferences and opportunities. In a market, these data come to decision makers automatically in the form of bid and asked prices, and the sincerity of the bidder never needs to be questioned. No such mechanism is available without the use of pricing and private, transferable rights.

We have spoken of economic efficiency and the bureaucratic pathologies involved in the reduction of environmental quality. How might an institutional reformation serve the interests of preservationists and environmentalists while at the same time increasing the efficiency of resource utilization and the sensitivity with which resources are harvested or extracted?

PROPERTY RIGHTS, SENSITIVITY, AND ENVIRONMENTAL STEWARDSHIP

Environmentalists fought the Sagebrush Rebellion knowing that a successful rebellion would conflict with their interests, recognizing that timber sheds are also amenity sheds and that these uses often conflict. Environmentalists have perceived resource development and extraction as the basic problems; and despite its record of environmental atrocities, federal management was viewed as preferable to state control. Yet this faith in existing institutions is unfounded. America's dependence on foreign sources for strategic minerals provides a good beginning for discussing how private property rights could benefit the causes of wilderness advocates and preservationists.

America is almost totally dependent on foreign sources for at least a dozen essential minerals and for more than 50 percent of half a dozen other essential minerals.[10] Over 90 percent of the columbite,

10. *U.S. News and World Report*, 12 November 1979, p. 75. See also *Background Papers: Draft for Public Review and Comment of the Report on Nonfuel Minerals Policy Review* (Washington, D.C.: U.S. Department of the Interior, August 1979); Report by the Comptroller General to the Congress of the United States, *The U.S. Mining and Mineral-Processing Industry: An Analysis of Trends and Implications* (Washington, D.C.: Govern-

strontium, titanium, manganese, chromite, and cobalt used in this country are supplied by sources outside the United States. Further, most of the sources of these minerals are politically unstable or potentially hostile countries. Manganese, for example, comes mainly from the Soviet Union and South Africa. Cobalt is imported primarily from Zaire, where 65 percent of the noncommunist world reserve is located. The major chromium deposits are in South Africa, Zimbabwe, and the Soviet Union. Given the limited short-run potentials for substitution, our high technology society is extremely dependent on these strategic minerals.[11]

A relatively high percentage of the land in mineral-rich states is in the public domain: 95 percent in Alaska, 86 percent in Nevada, 66 percent in Utah, and 64 percent in Idaho.[12] In 1977 the Department of Interior reported that 42 percent of the public lands was closed to hard rock mineral activity, 16 percent was severely restricted, and another 10 percent was moderately restricted.[13] One of the major problems with this trend, as seen by J. Allen Overton, president of the American Mining Congress, is that "the overwhelming part of these lands was never adequately evaluated for mineral potential."[14]

In the case of wilderness designation, there could be significant opportunity costs involved. When minerals are not extracted from protected lands, society pays the price in goods that are not produced and in higher prices for goods that are produced. Wilderness designation is a transfer activity similar to any other governmental program that involves a redistribution of wealth. In this case, society pays the opportunity costs so that the individuals who enjoy the wilderness can reap the benefits.

Those who use wilderness areas for recreation, or who simply obtain psychological satisfaction from knowing that they exist, benefit directly from this transfer activity. As in other transfers of wealth generated through the political process, the recipients of the transfer tend to be concentrated in well-organized groups, while those who pay the price tend to be diffuse and not identifiable as a coherent

ment Accounting Office, 1979); and James A. Miller, Daniel L. Fine, and Daniel McMichael, eds., *The Resource War in 3-D: Dependency, Diplomacy, Defense* (Pittsburgh: World Affairs Council, 1980).

11. *Wall Street Journal*, 26 February 1979, p. 24.

12. Public Land Law Review Commission, *One Third of the Nation's Land* (Washington, D.C.: Government Printing Office, 1970), pp. 121-38.

13. Comptroller General, *U.S. Mining and Mineral-Processing Industry*.

14. J. Allen Overton, quoted in Tony Velocci, "Minerals: The Resource Gap," *Nation's Business* 68 (October 1980): 36.

group. The perceived cost to the mass of individuals who pay for wilderness is small when compared to the benefits enjoyed by each user of the wilderness.

Environmentalists, preservationists, and wilderness buffs have seen the Sagebrush Rebellion as a threat rather than as an opportunity. The threat to wilderness preservation is that national policy could change drastically in the face of politically induced constraints on the supply of strategic minerals. Senator Harrison Schmitt, aware of ecological and economic concerns, has suggested the possibility of basic changes in national land policy. He asked, "As Soviet and other forces in the world gradually restrict or control our access to world energy and mineral resources, the question that wilderness advocates must answer is: 'Will they then advocate reopening Alaska and other federally controlled lands for rapid exploration and development in the national interest, when the national interest so dictates?' "[15]

The events of November 1973 suggest that environmental concerns can be quickly swept aside when the United States runs low on vital resources. The political railroading of the Alaskan pipeline is still a troubling memory for many of us. Ideally, the economic costs of any ecologically motivated action should be taken into account. But we should also have the ecological cost of any economically motivated action included in our calculus. The best hope of fulfilling both of these objectives lies in the institution of private property rights.

The Audubon Society is concerned with environmental quality in general and wildlife habitat in particular (see also chapter 4).[16] Once again, it is instructive to examine the society's management of the Rainey Wildlife Sanctuary in Vermilion Parish, Louisiana. The refuge is carefully controlled and managed for wildlife and for oil wells.

Because the Rainey Preserve is in private hands, there is every incentive to use the resource efficiently. The timing, placement, operation, and structure of the oil operation is carefully programmed with the seasonal requirements of the wildlife residents. Revenue from the operation is used to buy additional preserves and achieve Audubon Society goals. Clearly, this is a positive sum game. All participants win: The birds and wildlife have their habitat preserved, the public gets its oil, and Audubon receives revenues to purchase addi-

---

15. Senator Harrison Schmitt, quoted in ibid.

16. For more on this, see John Baden and Richard Stroup, "Saving the Wilderness: A Radical Proposal," *Reason* 13 (July 1981): 28–36.

tional preserves. The outcome is a function of property rights that leads to cooperative and efficient behavior.

Even though Audubon Society places fairly stringent controls on the activities of oil companies operating on the preserve, there appears to be no evidence that either the companies or the Audubon Society has experienced any major problems. As John "Frosty" Anderson, director of Audubon's Sanctuaries Department, stated, "The relationships we have had with oil companies . . . have been very satisfactory. As long as we know what precautions we want them to take, we have had no trouble in getting them to comply. . . . The companies have leaned over backwards." Lonnie Legé, manager of the Rainey Sanctuary, gives the Consolidated Oil and Gas Company, one of three oil companies operating on the marsh, credit for "improving by tenfold the capacity of certain areas of the marsh to sustain wildlife."[17]

Contrast Audubon's actions on their own lands with the society's pronouncements against exploration on the public lands. The difference in harmony between political and market decision making is extreme.

AN ALTERNATIVE

By its very nature, the mining of strategic minerals must be concentrated if it is to pay. In the United States, less than one million acres have been mined for nonfuel minerals in the last fifty years, and 90 percent of the free world's mineral requirements are supplied by less than twelve hundred mines. A small area of wilderness land used for mineral production might make a tremendous difference in terms of America's mineral independence. It is clearly inefficient to lock up such areas when a relatively insignificant portion of that land could yield huge mineral wealth and possibly strengthen national security. But at the same time that Gary Bennethum and J. Courtland Lee of the Department of Interior report that the federal government has withdrawn two-thirds of the nation's land from mining entry, politically active representatives become increasingly agitated.[18]

17. Ibid., p. 34.
18. Gary Bennethum and L. Courtland Lee, "Is Our Account Overdrawn?" *Mining Congress Journal* (September 1975), pp. 33–48.

It is unlikely that many large mineral deposits would be in areas of critical environmental concern. Those lands that have a high economic but a low ecological value should clearly be made available for development. Conversely, those with high ecological but low economic value should be left alone in a market setting. It would be especially beneficial if areas with both ecological and economic importance were managed by groups with the expertise to weigh the potential damage to the environment against the potential profits. Making environmental groups the owners (residual claimants able to garner any benefits they generate via added resource values) of the holdings would accomplish this end. Under these conditions, it is likely that other environmental interest groups would emulate the Audubon Society on the Rainey Preserve.

Assume that wilderness and restricted land is transferred in fee simple terms to an environmental interest group. The organization would then have the opportunity to lease the mineral rights and obtain the royalties. How would the organization behave? Assuming that the managers and directors of the interest group are intelligent and dedicated, they will attempt, in accordance with their values, to maximize the potential value of the resource. Assuming that they have a general interest in wilderness values and are not totally oriented toward any specific land area, they will carefully evaluate the contribution that this land could make to their goals.

For example, if the area has a titanium deposit that is expected to yield a million dollars worth of net benefits, they would consider developing it. Three basic questions would guide their decision. How much profit would such an activity yield? How much additional wilderness land or services could be bought with that profit? Is there a way to manage these lands that would permit mineral extraction while minimizing the impact on the wilderness features of the land; that is, how can the value of the joint products be maximized?

With fee simple title to the land, the wilderness group is forced to consider the opportunity costs of total nondevelopment. Rather than blindly opposing the extraction of commercially valuable resources from the land, the group must focus on obtaining these resources while maintaining the wilderness character of the area to an optimal degree. Different incentives lead to different behavior.

This change in the rules of the federal mineral game could yield enormous benefits. With land in private hands, all interested parties would become more constructive in their thinking and in their language. Instead of discrediting the goals of others, they would be concerned with how desired ends could be best achieved at the least cost to others. The owner would think this way in order to capture more revenues, selling off the highest valued package of rights consistent with his own goods. Similarly, a buyer of rights to mine or a buyer of conservation easements would want to purchase his valued package at the least cost to the seller and thus to himself. In addition, the unlimited wants of every party would be forced into priority classes. The *most important* land rights would be purchased, making claims that every contested acre is priceless suitably absurd.

Even people in single-minded pursuit of profits or of narrow wilderness goals would act *as if* other social goals mattered. Indeed, they may seek out higher valued uses of their own acreage, using profits to obtain new means to satisfy their own narrow goals. After all, it is their actions, not the worthiness of their goals, that concern the rest of society.

The basic problems that prompted the Sagebrush Rebellion and that might be substantially ameliorated by the above proposal are institutional, and their solution requires fundamental reform. Again, in this case as in others we examine, there is reason to be optimistic. First, however, the myths must be destroyed and an understanding constructed.

Chapter 9

TIMBER BEASTS, TREE HUGGERS, AND THE OLD FOLKS AT HOME

Prior to the establishment of the Forest Service, loggers acted as though timber had little value, cutting out one area and moving to another without replanting.[1] This "cut and get out" approach can be understood if examined in the context of the time. Wood was plentiful, the standing inventory of timber was huge, and trees often had a negative value. Under these conditions, it did not make sense to invest resources in growing more trees. As trees began to increase in monetary value, many influential people failed to understand that timber—like other commodities—responds to market forces. Because it was feared that timber was becoming irreversibly scarce, the federal government got into the business of growing and managing commercial resources—and everyone has paid the cost.

There are two major problems with public timber management. First, the U.S. Forest Service systematically supports inefficient timber production. Instead of investing the nation's resources where the marginal returns are the highest, the Forest Service is influenced by political considerations only haphazardly related to site productivity. The agency engages in accounting practices, such as the allowable cut effect, that distort and inflate reported returns on invest-

---

1. For a further discussion of forestlands regulation, see the Pacific Institute volume entitled *Forestlands: Public and Private*, ed. M. Bruce Johnson and Robert Deacon (Cambridge, Mass.: Ballinger, forthcoming).

ments. By maximizing the volume of extractions from a site rather than seeking the efficiency potential of that site, the Forest Service has deprived the nation of billions of board feet of timber each year.

The second problem involves environmental quality. In essence, the Forest Service has forced taxpayers to underwrite the costs of logging uneconomical sites. For years, citizens have paid the difference between the costs of logging and the value of the products hauled from the woods. Every time this occurs, the public quite literally subsidizes the reduction of environmental quality.

If our timber resources were managed efficiently in terms of economic and environmental criteria, we would have more timber at lower prices *and* more wilderness and back country recreation. Under ideal conditions, the specialist in timber management would dominate the highly productive sites. The Weyerhausers and Boise Cascades of the world have little interest in tying up their investments on land with little commercial value, so most of the lands would be available for dispersed recreation, grazing, and watershed provision.

What are the possibilities and consequences of imposing private property rights on much of our public timber lands? Following on the heels of the environmental decade, in the 1980s we confront the reality checks of increasing scarcity caused by poor management. It is time to dispel another misconception.

The 1970s transported us from the dreams of Camelot and the Great Society to the realization that we face serious synergistic problems. Three of these problems are particularly important: (1) lagging productivity, (2) continuing concern with environmental quality, and (3) a looming crisis in the Social Security system. Declining economic productivity and growth rates are blamed on increasing natural resource scarcities, governmental policies relating to the environment, and high tax rates. Environmental concerns spring from "too much attention to economic growth at the expense of the environment" as well as plain mismanagement. The stupendous actuarial deficit of the Social Security system is seen as requiring either large increases in tax rates or the breaking of explicit and implicit promises made to current and future retirees.

The sobering up period that followed the giddy days of the 1960s taught Americans that not all good things go together. Nevertheless, the problems cited above can be attacked simultaneously. It is possible to increase natural resource availability, conserve environmental quality, ensure labor productivity, and make present and future retirees financially secure. In other words, the timber beasts, the tree huggers, and the old folks at home can all be made better off.

If our plan is adopted, there should be an increasing demand for silviculturists and wildlife biologists and a decreasing demand for lobbyists, lawyers, and those skilled in alarmist rhetoric. People in the last three groups commonly specialize in transferring wealth, resources, and income to special interest groups. They have been directing our economic traffic for so long and we have gone so far down their road that only a fundamental change in institutions can bring us back on the path of strong economic growth and toward a *constructive* implementation of environmental awareness. Our plan should also reduce the negative sum games and the divisiveness that characterize U.S. Forest Service policy.

The key to our plan is a shift of responsibility for roughly one-third of our nation's land away from the political and into the private sector. Day-to-day management would be taken from public bureaucrats and given to private sector employees. In most cases, these employees would be the same people who currently toil in the bowels of the bureaucracy. They are generally both creative and competent, including those who pull the tangle of strings that controls the bureaucracy. If each decision maker is given more responsibility for specific assets, there is good reason to believe that both attitudes and performances will improve dramatically.

FEDERAL TIMBER: UNPRICED SERVICES AND MISMANAGED FORESTS

The federal government has managerial responsibility for approximately one-third of the nation's land. Much of that land, 187,819,000 acres, is forested,[2] with a total of 107,109,000 acres considered commercial forest.[3] Even without imaginative management initiatives, this commercial timberland is worth hundreds of billions of dollars. Like a farm, the value of a commercial forest is comprised of the value of the standing crop plus the discounted value

2. U.S., Department of Agriculture, *Agricultural Statistics, 1979* (Washington, D.C.: Government Printing Office, 1979), p. 539.

3. U.S., Department of Agriculture, Forest Service, *The Outlook for Timber in the United States*, Forest Resource Report no. 20 (Washington, D.C.: Government Printing Office, October 1973), p. 11.

of future crops. When the current wheat crop is harvested, for example, the value of the farm does not drop to zero. The same logic applies to commercial forest land.

The overwhelming majority of federally owned commercial timberland is managed by the U.S. Forest Service in the Department of Agriculture and the BLM in the Department of Interior. Under federal statute, public timberlands are to be managed for multiple use and sustained yield. They are explicitly *not* to be managed to maximize net revenue. Thus, estimates of unpriced recreation, wildlife grazing, and water production are included as valued outputs when management decisions are made. Unfortunately, under current arrangements, it is difficult to manage these lands efficiently. The managers lack information regarding the relative values of competing products, and trade-offs must constantly be made among recreation, logging, wildlife, and livestock grazing uses.

If the public forests are to yield a maximum net contribution to social welfare, public managers must sensitively discover and produce a changing mix of products. Clearly, the appropriate management strategy would be different if the demand for forest products were very low rather than very high, but the relative value of alternative products shifts over time and varies from one place to another. If each product were marketed, however, managers could respond efficiently to changing demands.

Most knowledgeable people agree that federal agencies systematically fail to produce an optimal mix of products.[4] In the absence of information provided by prices, their task is virtually impossible. Because decisions are made on the basis of biased information and incentives generated by the existing institutional framework, it would be naive to expect socially optimal managerial decisions. Thus, the solution to poor management lies in institutional reform, not in firing incompetent people or in hiring better ones.

Biased information is used in managing the public forest partly because many services are unpriced or are priced arbitrarily. Recreation is probably the classic example. Information is received from the public through hearings, letters, and so forth, but it is difficult to judge their intensity or validity. Unlike the buyer who personally makes the choice between one good or service and another, the citi-

---

4. A concise summary of management problems in national forests can be found in ibid., pp. 762–67.

zen who demands public services does not give up what society must sacrifice in order to provide them.

Are such demands valid? Are they overstated? In reality, most of the demands for national forest services are simply unstated. On most policy matters, voters are rationally ignorant (see chapter 4).[5] Since many citizens cannot identify the services they may want in the future and since they recognize that their voices will have little effect anyway, many demands are typically unvoiced. This contrasts sharply to what happens in markets, where each buyer pays for what he gets, and entrepreneurs or speculators gain wealth by correctly anticipating future demands and supplying them.

When all items carry a price that correctly states their opportunity costs, individuals in a market system based on property rights and willing exchange will systematically move resources to their most highly valued uses. Prices provide condensed information on relative values along with incentives to act on that information. In the private sector, decision makers have an incentive (e.g., personal wealth or income) to seek out rather than to ignore these data.

When the relevant facts (prices) are distributed among those affected, prices foster the coordination of a vast number of people. For example, assume that tomorrow a widely demanded new use is found for Port Orford cedar, a tree used to produce wooden pencils. With an increase in the demand and a set (short-run) supply, the price will increase. Some users may know all the facts, others may believe that students have started smoking cedar shavings because of their aphrodisiac properties, while others may believe that Mt. St. Helens buried the forest under one hundred feet of ash. From the users' perspective, the cause of increased relative scarcity is irrelevant. The important thing is that the signal and the incentive to conserve are received.

In marked contrast, centralized bureaucracies maximize the information requirements. For example, if more Port Orford cedar is to be harvested than previously planned, then a great many people must be consulted. We cannot simply trust a Forest Service manager to make the right decision. He does not have full information on all alternatives. Further, if he lowers the value of the forest, the *public* wealth, not his own, suffers. Thus a great number of checks and bal-

5. James Gwartney and Richard Stroup, *Economics: Private and Public Choice* (New York: Academic Press, 1980), chaps. 4 and 31.

ances (sometimes called red tape) must be in place. Those whose interests are slightly injured may have veto power over any such change, and those who are harmed a great deal may not be heard from if they have no organization or spokesperson.

There is yet another problem. Most forests were never explicitly purchased by the controlling agency, and the enormous value they represent is not shown as a cost on the agency's books. For example, holding old growth timber off the market while it physically declines is a genuine social loss that does not appear as a cost to agency decision makers. It is simply ignored. This is unlikely in a private forest. Consider the case of someone who inherits a forest with all taxes paid. At first it might seem that it costs that person nothing to hold the forest, but on closer examination we realize that one cost of holding the land is the need to reject the highest bid made by whoever else might want the land. That is a clear loss, exactly equal in size to what others are willing to pay for the resource being held off the auction block.

In sum, the bid and asked prices of goods and services and the asset value of a forest provide signals and incentives to private forest owners and managers. In the public sector, such prices and values are commonly missing or can simply be ignored, since there is no residual claimant (i.e., one in authority who personally gains by moving the resource to a higher valued use). In addition, since the personal wealth of the decision maker is not at stake, we must impose artificial accountability constraints (e.g., red tape) on the decision process.

Problems in National Forest Management

Until about twenty years ago, the life of a national forest administrator, whether the regional forester, the forest supervisor, or the district ranger, was relatively simple and pleasant. The demands for recreation and other amenity services from the forest were comparatively easy to satisfy. Producer groups included primarily logging operations and livestock owners, and conflicts were minor. But rising incomes and mobility led to an increase in the demand for forest recreation; and as the demand for environmental quality increased, new conflicts were generated and old ones intensified.

The demand for trees and forage increased along with the demand to drill for oil and to dig for minerals. The ownership of recreational vehicles, from four-wheel drives to motor homes, exploded, and off-road vehicles swarmed through the forest. At the same time, membership was soaring in the Wilderness Society and the Sierra Club.[6] Environmental groups advocated a near total moratorium on anything but nature walks and photography, and their cries were competing more and more with the roar of the chainsaw. And the forest manager was caught in the middle.

As the debate grew more heated, the so-called wisdom of the experts and the voice of the public were increasingly summoned. Formal planning, public hearings, and litigation turned the lives of many foresters from an idyll into a nightmare. Berated by experts, powerful special interest groups, and factions of the general public, the forester was condemned no matter what he did.

Nobel prize-winning economist Friedrich A. Hayek has shown in elegant, theoretical detail why efficient public planning is a logical impossibility.[7] The coordination of even a small part of the economy cannot be efficiently accomplished in the absence of prices determined through the free trade of private property rights. In sum, there is no substitute for the time- and location-specific knowledge that each individual possesses in carefully considering the available and acceptable trade-offs.

Hayek's work was theoretical. In the real world of the besieged bureaucrat, increased demands for forest products lead to more intense planning efforts. The forestry teams who attempt to compare the apples and oranges of alternative forest outputs, to evaluate unpriced services from the forest, and to develop rules that can apply throughout the forest system (if not the nation) must confront the nasty reality checks that correspond to the generalized world of Hayek's theories.

Even the most skilled team of foresters, biologists, engineers, archeologists, landscape architects, wildlife managers, hydrologists, social scientists, computer programmers, and other experts cannot duplicate the coordination provided by the amazingly complex prices (and simplicity of result) of price structures. When each resource user surveys the options available and bids for the use of particular mixes of resources, the high bids convey a vast array of condensed

6. John Baden, ed., *Earth Day Reconsidered* (Washington, D.C.: Heritage Foundation, 1980), chap. 3.

7. F. A. Hayek, "The Use of Knowledge and Society," *American Economic Review* 35 (September 1945): 519–30.

information on desires and options. The winning bids (market prices) thus replace armies of experts, public speakers, and litigants. Of course, there are well-known flaws in the market picture (that is, externalities, potential monopolies, and public goods), but compared to the information problems and distortions of the political process, market problems diminish to relative insignificance. A bit of tinkering on the margins will often suffice. Indeed, many market problems can either be solved by entrepreneurs who put together larger packages (e.g., a large resort development, where protective covenants enhance the developers' real estate values by protecting the ambience of the area), by the ingenuity of competitors seeking monopoly rents, or by government regulation of externalities or provision of public goods.

Planning versus Market Coordination

When well-trained economists look at the planning process, they see many problems in the way values are assigned, in the way criteria are set, and in the lack of distinction between the two.[8] These problems can be easily explained. They are caused by the lack of good data inherent in a failure to price outputs as well as inputs, in a failure to recognize the opportunity cost of capital, and to the pressures that must come to bear when decision makers are held accountable only through the political system. The wonder is that the national forests have been managed as well as they have.

Privatizing the national forests should end many of the obstacles to good management. Not only would decision makers be given larger amounts of validated and continuously updated information, but political obstacles to efficient management would largely disappear. Perhaps just as important, environmentalists, timber producers, miners, recreationists, and others who make demands on the Forest Service would quickly move away from their carping and faultfinding toward positive and constructive accommodation.

Whenever someone owns a piece of land, everyone with a potential interest in it begins to act *as if* they cared about everyone else. Each party's goals can best be reached by close, constructive, and even imaginative cooperation with all other parties. This results whenever trade occurs by the rule of willing consent, for such trade must be

8. Clawson, "The National Forests," p. 762.

mutually beneficial. This process contrasts sharply with debates over public land, where the name of the game is discrediting the other side's views and rejecting compromises unless defeat appears imminent. When the price is zero, each side naturally wants it all.

SOCIAL SECURITY: THE CONCEPT
AND THE REALITY

We turn now to a problem even larger in scope than that of national forest mismanagement, Social Security. The tax wedge of the payroll tax necessary to support the Social Security system has increased enormously over the last few years. More than half of all workers now pay more Social Security tax than federal income tax. Promises made by politicians eager to buy the votes of older Americans—a group that votes more consistently than any other segment of the population—have resulted in an actuarial deficit estimated to be somewhere between enormous and incredible.

The Social Security system was created in 1935 in an economic environment of high unemployment, little investment demand, and low personal income tax rates. It was originally presented to the public as a conservative pension system that would provide support to the elderly and induce them to leave the labor force, thus opening up jobs for the rest of the population. Stressing an "earned" benefit made the program acceptable to conservatives. "Contributions were to be paid by the worker and the employer into a trust fund; interest was to be credited on trust fund balances; and benefits were formally to be based on workers' previous earnings."[9]

The first taxes were collected in 1937 at the rate of 2 percent of earnings, up to a maximum of sixty dollars, split evenly between employer and employee. Though benefits were to begin in 1942, Congress amended the legislation to begin payments in 1940. This meant that fully 98 percent of the benefits was unearned for a single male retiring at age sixty-five in 1940 after only three years in the system. Even by 1970, 68 percent of the benefits paid to the retiring male was unearned.[10] One might conclude that it was planned that benefit

9. Lawrence C. Davis, "Progress Toward Efficiency in National Forest Management," *Cato Journal*, forthcoming.

10. Joseph A. Pechman, "The Social Security System: An Overview," in *The Crisis in Social Security: Problems and Prospects*, ed. Michael J. Boskin (San Francisco: Institute for Contemporary Studies, 1977), p. 32.

levels would exceed the actuarial value of contributions, thus resulting in an intergenerational transfer of income through the federal
government—a way of having the working-age population contribute
to the support of the aged.[11]

In the early years of the program, payers vastly outnumbered recipients. Because the cost was low, workers scarcely noticed the bur-
den, however, and grateful older people loved the politicians who
supported the program. It was a political dream. The problems would
occur in the future.

In 1940 the system was already on a pay-as-you-go basis. Only a
small cash reserve, euphemistically called a trust fund, was main-
tained to help level fluctuations between income and outgo.[12] The
absolute size of the welfare component of Social Security is high,
rivaling in size all other federal, state, and local public assistance
programs.[13]

By the late 1970s, close to 90 percent of all employees in the
United States were covered by Social Security. By 1981 the original
tax had increased to 13.3 percent, and 6.65 percent was withheld
from paychecks on the first $29,700 of earnings. We have gone from
a maximum of $30 per year withheld from earnings to $1,975.05—a
6,500 percent increase. The Social Security Act Amendments of
1977 provided for a tax increase that will push the rate to 15.3
percent by 1990 and will raise the current ceiling on taxable earnings
to almost $32,000 by the early 1980s. Thereafter it will increase as
average earnings increase.[14] Thirty-five million individuals are currently receiving benefits at a cost of $10 billion a month. This money
is being paid into the system at approximately the same rate by 114
million taxpayers.[15]

In the forty-odd years since the inception of Social Security, the
economic and demographic environment has changed, but the Social
Security program has remained essentially the same. Today's tight
labor market, capital scarcity, and high personal tax rates call for a

11. Donald O. Parsons and Douglas R. Munro, "Intergenerational Transfers in Social
Security," in ibid., p. 84.

12. Charles M. Platt, "Social Security: Will It Be There When You Need It?" *U.S. News*
86 (30 April 1979): 25.

13. Parsons and Munro, "Intergenerational Transfers," p. 66.

14. Ibid., p. 61.

15. Michael J. Boskin, "Social Security and the Economy," in *The United States in the
1980s*, ed. Peter Duignan and Alvin Rabushka (Stanford, Calif.: Hoover Institution Press,
1980), p. 183.

different approach—one that does not impede employment and capital formation.[16] A system that encourages early retirement and discourages savings can only exacerbate the problems. The transfer or pay-as-you-go component of Social Security has, according to some estimates, reduced the national savings rate by 50 percent and may thus be responsible for our low level of real investment. As a result, our economy is becoming much less productive compared with nations such as Germany and Japan, whose personal savings rate as a percent of income is several times higher than in the United States.[17] American productivity suffers accordingly. What is to be done?

If a younger generation decides it can't pay the bill for the older, there will be a crisis of major proportions. One suggestion for solving the impending deficit is to permit funding out of general revenues. But this solution only hides the real cost of Social Security and precludes the necessary reform of the system. Only a highly visible, earmarked tax will send the needed signals to the public, the Congress, and the executive branch. Furthermore, any transfer from general revenues would still necessitate either tax increases or further budget deficits—both to the detriment of the country. This no-win situation would either increase income taxes or cause skyrocketing inflation.

Funding from general revenues has been only one of the patchwork solutions suggested recently. Other short- and long-term solutions include:

1. Gradually increasing Social Security taxes from 12.26 percent in 1980 to 15.30 percent in 1990.
2. Gradually increasing the wage base on which the tax is paid.
3. Increasing the amount of money Social Security beneficiaries may earn without having their benefits reduced.
4. Increasing retirement age in small increments over a number of years to 68.
5. Combining the three trust funds to allow greater flexibility for timing additional financing.
6. Reducing benefits.
7. Eliminating minimum benefits.
8. Removing earnings tests for retirees.

16. Alvin Rabushka and Bruce Jacobs quoted in Lindley H. Clark Jr., "Help for the Elderly: A Need for a Focus," *The Wall Street Journal*, 2 March 1981, p. 1.

17. Martin Feldstein, ed., *The American Economy in Transition* (Chicago: University of Chicago Press, 1980), p. 4.

9. Taxing Social Security income.
10. Compelling federal employees to participate.
11. Preventing withdrawals of state and local governments.
12. Finding alternatives to Social Security and placing more reliance on private pension and insurance plans.

Out of the many suggestions and schemes for reform, one fact remains clear: Constructive change cannot be put off. To avert a crisis, we need to consider both short- and long-term solutions and then apply some creative thinking to the process. Change will not be easy. For substantial, meaningful reform, the general public and Congress must be informed and mobilized. If the nation waits until the tax bite sends us that information, it will be too late.

For equity and political reasons, we must honor our current obligations. But a strong argument can be made for a voluntary system with alternative private insurance and pension programs. Under this system, some form of minimum old-age insurance would be mandatory, but each individual or employer would have the freedom to make the choice as to carrier. This program would be a true insurance program where individual payments would purchase an equivalent amount in actuarial benefits. The tax wedge problem disappears when every dollar paid in by a worker is expected to buy benefits for the same worker. The welfare aspects of Social Security would be financed out of the general revenues to the extent that the nation found affordable and desirable. There would no longer be confusion between an earned entitlement and welfare.

To carry the nation through the changeover period and to compensate the generation whose contributions have already been spent but who are about to retire, we propose that commercial timberlands in the national forests be sold. This could eliminate both the current mismanagement of timberlands and the rising deficit in the Social Security program. The advantages inherent in private property rights, including the efficient management of natural resources, would apply. This one move could reduce government bureaucracy and taxes and put vast natural resources to their most highly valued uses.

Privatizing the National Forests:
A Modest Proposal

We have elsewhere suggested that changes in federal law could make land management decisions more responsible.[18] We have suggested that large chunks of federal land be given in fee simple terms to established conservation groups. We believe that it does not matter very much who owns a resource when it comes to determining how that resource will be used. Any owner, whatever his goals, will find those goals frequently met more fully by cooperation with others through trade. Since dollars, additional wilderness lands, buffer zones for existing wilderness, and other items attainable through trade are desired by any potential owner, it follows that even a zealot who owns the land can gain by listening carefully and discussing constructively the alternatives proposed by nonowners who desire wilderness, mineral, or other values from the landowner. Until all rights are (for the moment) optimally allocated among competing and compatible uses and users, further trade can make all parties to the trade better off in the pursuit of their various goals.

In this same spirit, we suggest that a realistic solution to the forest productivity problem as well as a major attack on the labor productivity and the Social Security deficit problems would be possible if the national forests were sold. At the same time, the federal Social Security program could be made voluntary, permitting carefully monitored private alternatives.[19] Existing Social Security obligations

18. See John Baden and Richard Stroup, eds., *Bureaucracy vs. Environment: The Environmental Costs of Bureaucratic Governance* (Ann Arbor: University of Michigan Press, 1981); idem, "Transgenerational Equity and Natural Resources: Or, Too Bad We Don't Have Coal Rangers," in ibid., pp. 203–16; idem, "Environmental Quality, Social Welfare, and Bureaucratic Pathologies," in *Earth Day Reconsidered*, ed. John Baden (Washington, D.C.: Heritage Foundation, 1980), pp. 33–42; idem, "Conversations with the Beyond: A Negative Tax on Speculative Profits," *Taxing and Spending* 3 (Summer 1980): 3; idem, "Property Rights and Natural Resource Management," *Literature of Liberty* 2 (October–December 1979): 4; idem, "An Integrated Approach to National Forest Management: Response to Krutilla and Haigh," *Environmental Law* (Winter 1978); idem, "Property Rights, Environmental Quality, and the Management of National Forests," in *Managing the Commons*, ed. Garrett Hardin and John Baden (San Francisco: W.H. Freeman, 1977); idem, "Private Rights, Public Choices, and the Management of National Forests," *Western Wildlands* (Autumn 1975), pp. 5–13; idem, "Externality, Property Rights and the Management of Our National Forests," *Journal of Law and Economics* (April 1974).

19. Of course the very existence of any social security program on an involuntary basis is paternalistic and logically open to challenge on that basis. We assume, however, the political necessity for such a mandatory program.

could be met largely from proceeds from the forest sale. Both the weight of theory and the bulk of available evidence suggest that the interests of those desiring maximum production of material goods from the forests, those concerned with amenities in the environment, and those demanding that we keep promises to our older citizens could all be advanced considerably.

Clearly, the sale of commercial timberlands from the national forests should be gradual. Early sales would provide solid evidence of both potential revenues and the degree of potential improvement in management. Since the values of timber, minerals, and amenity sheds all fluctuate with time and the economy, bids on any portion of the forest system would fluctuate as well. Like a conservative investor constructing a stock portfolio, the averaging process brought about by gradual sales would reduce the element of chance in the production of revenue. In addition, gradual sales would ensure that prices would not be artificially driven down by large and temporary gluts on the market.

The size of plots to be sold is another important consideration. It is vital that the plots be large enough to allow private planning, especially where amenities are involved. When large investors, clubs, partnerships, and corporations can purchase tracts large enough to incorporate what otherwise would be external effects, then the externalities are internalized. The purchasing firm is able to use restrictive covenants where necessary to maximize the value of the total land package and then sell off in smaller pieces whatever is not necessary to its own plans. This is commonly done in setting up large resorts. The integrity of the land use plan is preserved. This is simply the "planned unit development" concept applied in a forested setting.

The point is that if a mining company bought an entire forest, it would have every incentive to maximize the value of the 98 percent that it didn't really want by carefully considering the amenity effects of its exploration and mining operations. Similarly, if the Audubon Society submitted the high bid on ecologically critical portions of all the resold part of the forest, it would carefully consider its information and preferences. Demanding more only increases the required bid. The major reason we expect improvement in forest management is that a market system holds every private owner accountable to the rest of society by having to outbid everyone else—or reject others' bids—for every alternative forgone (or destroyed) on the land.

It is easy to see how the private ownership system fosters cooperation. Each party wants to get or meet its own desires at *minimum
cost* to itself and thus must think in terms of what others want. But
what about the individual who does not want to buy a part of the
national forest but still wants access? Consider what people from
Montana do when they want to use facilities in New York City but
do not want to purchase real estate there. Just as some of the living
space in New York is rented by the day or by the month, some of
the private land in our country is leased by the hour, the week, or
the year. Some people will pay a higher price for vacations filled with
amenities, and many owners of the world's resources are happy to
accommodate such vacationers. Access to a unique ecological site
may be compared with access to a Rembrandt painting. In both
cases, the admission fee can make it worthwhile for the owner to
share the asset and, indeed, take elaborate precautions against its
depreciation.

A key feature of our proposal is that the immense forest wealth of
our nation would be more broadly shared among all citizens. Instead
of a few favored firms and individuals enjoying the benefits of the
forest, everyone would benefit from the revenues. Those revenues
would capture the high bidder's estimate of the present capitalized
value of all future benefits that could be derived from the land.

How large would the revenues from the sale of the national forests be? No one really knows. But it is not the *average* person's
value that would determine the sale price of any tract. It is, rather,
the most optimistic view, shared by the minimum number of people
necessary to win the auction for a piece of land. Indeed, the winning bid would reflect a composite of the most optimistic bids, since
interests in each large tract would tend to be subdivided, with relevant precautions taken by means of protective covenants in order to
enhance each parcel's value. In short, the value of the land, as of all
other private land, would be held down only by the limits to the
imagination of the most optimistic bidders.

Marion Clawson estimated that the national forests were worth
$42 billion in 1976.[20] Since then there have been large increases in
timber prices, in the value of strategic minerals, and in the value of
oil and gas potential. In addition, the demand for recreation opportunities and amenity values continues to increase. With reduced op-

20. Clawson, "The National Forests."

portunities for "free" forest services, we would expect prices to rise significantly. Note, however, that this does *not* mean that the average citizen, or even the forest user, is necessarily disadvantaged. Currently, every citizen is a member of one of the most expensive clubs in the world: the U.S. Forest Service. Our club dues are measured in tax dollars paid and in productivity values forgone. With the constructive attitudes and imaginative entrepreneurship unleashed by implementation of our proposal, the national forests could be sold for several hundred billion dollars.

This revenue would be a great beginning toward reforming the Social Security system. If each worker were given a choice of an actuarial, sound Social Security investment or the best available private alternative, then the tax rate associated with retirement and medical security could be dramatically lowered. That is, each worker might continue to put aside the same amount as he currently pays in taxes, but each would have a vested interest in what he pays for. The current system is largely a welfare system, so that most of the time workers gain little in the way of increased benefits if they choose to work with more intelligence, care, or diligence. Making the system actuarially sound would restore the connection between work effort and rewards received, the tax wedge would disappear, and employers and workers would no longer be punished for their productive efforts. An enormous debt has been built up and must somehow be paid off.

CONCLUSION

Making the pie bigger is what efficiency is all about; but it is also the only way to make everyone better off. Increased efficiency—that is, movement toward the production possibility frontier—is the only real source of a "free lunch." Efficient use of resources requires that decision makers have both the authority and the responsibility for the resources about which decisions are being made. A nationalized industry, whether in automobiles, the postal service, or the forest, will simply not be efficiently managed. Contrary to popular belief, the problems that result from nationalization are the fault of bad information and incentive systems, not bad people. When the worst cases of externalities can be controlled, private and transferable property rights are the best way to link responsibility and authority consistently.

Our proposal would help the American productivity problem in two important ways. First, it would make better use of the mineral, timber, recreation, and amenity values found in the public forests. Second, it would make possible a substantial reduction in the enormous tax wedge being driven between what employers pay and what employees receive for their work. Perhaps as important to the future of the nation would be a fundamental change in attitude. From the fierce and never-ending battles of lobbyist pressures and alarmist rhetoric would emerge a positive sum game. Rewards would be given for imaginative and constructive solutions to resource conflicts rather than for carefully articulated pleas and raw political clout. The formidable power of American entrepreneurs would be shifted from the negative sum political arena to the positive sum private arena, where every change must be mutually beneficial.

SELECTED BIBLIOGRAPHY

Ackerman, B.A., and Hassler, W.T. *Clean Coal/Dirty Air, or How the Clean-Air Act Became a Multibillion-Dollar Bail-Out for High Sulfur Coal Producers and What Should Be Done About It.* New Haven: Yale University Press, 1981.

Alchian, Armen, and Demsetz, Harold. "Property Rights Paradigm." *Journal of Economic History* 33 (March 1973).

Anderson, Frederick R.; Kneese, Allen V.; Reed, Phillip D.; Taylor, Serge; and Stevenson, Russell R. *Environmental Improvement Through Economic Incentives.* Baltimore: Johns Hopkins Press, 1977.

Anderson, Terry L., ed. *Water Rights: Scarce Resource Allocation, Bureaucracy, and the Environment.* Cambridge, Mass.: Ballinger and Pacific Institute for Public Policy Research, 1983.

Anderson, Terry L., and Hill, P.J. "The Evolution of Property Rights: A Study of the American West." *Journal of Law and Economics* 18 (April 1975): 163-79.

_____. "Toward a General Theory of Institutional Change." In *Frontiers of Economics*, pp. 3-18. Blacksburg, Va.: University Publications, 1976.

_____. *The Birth of a Transfer Society.* Stanford, Calif.: Hoover Institution Press, 1980.

_____. "Establishing Property Rights in Energy: Efficient vs. Inefficient Processes." *Cato Journal* 1 (1981): 87-105.

Angelides, S., and Bardach, E. *Water Banking: How to Stop Wasting Agricultural Water.* San Francisco: Institute for Contemporary Studies, 1978.

This selected bibliography was prepared with the assistance of Pacific Institute Research Fellow Gary D. Libecap, Associate Professor of Economics, Texas A&M University.

Armentano, D. T. "The Petroleum Industry: An Historical Study in Power." *Cato Journal* 1 (Spring 1981): 53–85.

Baden, John A., and Stroup, Richard L. "The Environmental Costs of Government Action." *Policy Review* (Spring 1978): 23–26.

_____. eds. *Bureaucracy Versus Environment: The Environmental Costs of Bureaucratic Governance.* Ann Arbor: University of Michigan Press, 1981.

_____. "Entrepreneurship, Energy, and the Political Economy of Hope." In *Exploration and Economics of the Petroleum Industry*, Proceedings of the Southwestern Legal Foundation, vol. 19, New York: Matthew Bender, 1981.

_____. "Externality, Property Rights, and the Management of Our National Forests." *Journal of Law and Economics* 16 (Spring 1973).

_____. "Property Rights and Natural Resource Management." *Literature of Liberty* 2 (October–December 1979): 5–44.

_____. "Saving the Wilderness: A Radical Proposal." *Reason* 13 (July 1981): 28–36.

_____, and Thurman, Walter. "Myths, Admonitions and Rationality: The American Indian as a Resource Manager." *Economic Inquiry* 19 (January 1981): 132–43.

Barlow, Thomas, et al. *Giving Away the National Forests: An Analysis of U.S. Forest Service Timber Sales Below Costs.* Washington, D.C.: Natural Resources Defense Council, 1980.

Batten, Charles R. "Toward a Free Market in Forest Resources." *Cato Journal* 1 (Fall 1981): 501–17.

Baumol, William J., and Oates, Wallace E. *Economics, Environmental Policy, and the Quality of Life.* Englewood Cliffs, N.J.: Prentice-Hall, 1979.

Beckwith, James P., Jr. "Parks, Property Rights, and the Possibilities of the Private Law." *Cato Journal* 1 (Fall 1981): 473–99.

Benson, Bruce L. "Why Are Congressional Committees Dominated by 'High Demand' Legislators?—A Comment on Niskanen's View of Bureaucrats and Politicians." *Southern Economic Journal* 48: 68–77.

Borcherding, T. E., ed. *Budgets and Bureaucrats: The Sources of Government Growth.* Durham, N.C.: Duke University Press, 1977.

Bottomley, Anthony. "The Effect of Common Ownership of Land Upon Resource Allocation in Tripolitania." *Land Economics* 39 (February 1963): 91–95.

Buchanan, James, and Tullock, Gordon. *The Calculus of Consent.* Ann Arbor: University of Michigan Press, 1962.

Burt, Oscar R. "Groundwater Management Under Institutional Restrictions." *Water Resources Research* 6 (1970): 1540–48.

Campbell, Colin D., ed. *Financing Social Security.* Washington, D.C.: American Enterprise Institute, 1979.

Cheung, Steven. "The Structure of a Contract and the Theory of a Non-Exclusive Resource." *Journal of Law and Economics* 3 (1970): 49–70.

Clawson, Marion. *The Bureau of Land Management.* New York: Praeger Publications, 1971.

_____ . "The Economics of National Forest Management." In *Resources for the Future,* Working Paper EN-6, Baltimore: Johns Hopkins Press, 1976.

_____ . *Forests: For Whom and For What?* Baltimore: Johns Hopkins Press, 1975.

_____ . "The National Forests." *Science* 191 (1976): 762-67.

_____ , and Held, Burnell. *The Federal Lands: Their Use and Management.* Baltimore: Johns Hopkins Press, 1957.

Coase, Ronald. "The Problem of Social Costs." *The Journal of Law and Economics* 4 (October 1960): 1-44.

Culhane, Paul J. *Public Lands Politics.* Baltimore: Johns Hopkins Press, 1981.

Cuzán, Alfred. "A Critique of Collectivist Water Resources Planning." *Western Political Quarterly* 32 (September 1979).

Dana, Samuel T., and Fairfax, Sally K. *Forest and Range Policy.* New York: McGraw-Hill, 1980.

Davis, Kenneth P. *Forest Management.* New York: McGraw-Hill, 1966.

De Alessi, Louis. "The Economics of Property Rights: A Review of the Evidence." *Research in Law and Economics* 2 (1980): 1-47.

Demsetz, Harold. "Some Aspects of Property Rights." *Journal of Law and Economics* 9 (October 1966): 61-70.

Dennis, William C. "The Public and Private Interest in Wilderness Protection." *Cato Journal* 1 (Fall 1981): 373-90.

DeVany, Arthur S. "Land Reform and Agricultural Efficiency in Mexico: A General Equilibrium Analysis." *Journal of Monetary Economics* 6 (1977) Suppl. Series: 123-47.

_____ , and Sanchez, Nicolas. "Land Tenure Structures and Fertility in Mexico." *Review of Economics and Statistics* 61 (February 1979): 67-72.

Duignan, Peter, and Rabushka, Alvin, eds. *The United States in the 1980s.* Stanford, Calif.: Hoover Institution Press, 1980.

Eckert, Ross D. "Regulatory Commission Behavior: Taxi Franchising in Los Angeles and Other Cities." Ph.D. thesis, Department of Economics, University of California, Los Angeles, 1968.

_____ . "On the Incentives of Regulators: The Case of Taxicabs." *Public Choice* 14 (Spring 1973): 83-100.

Edwards, Franklin R. "Managerial Objectives in Regulated Industries—Preference Behavior in Banking." *Journal of Political Economy* 85 (February 1977): 147-62.

Erickson, Edward W. "United States Energy Policy: The Translucent Hand and the Art of Muddling Through." *Cato Journal* 1 (Fall 1981): 609-27.

Feldstein, Martin, ed. *The American Economy in Transition.* Chicago: University of Chicago Press, 1980.

Frech, Harry E. III. "The Property Rights Theory of the Firm: Empirical Results from a Natural Experiment." *Journal of Political Economy* 84 (February 1976): 143–52.

———. "Health Insurance: Private, Mutuals, or Government." In *The Economics of Nonproprietary Organization*, edited by Kenneth W. Clarkson and Donald L. Martin, pp. 61–73, Supplement to vol. 1, *Research in Law and Economics*, 1979.

Furubotn, Eirik. "Bank Credit and the Labor-managed Firm: The Yugoslav Case." In *The Economics of Property Rights*, edited by E. G. Furubotn and S. Pejovich. Cambridge, Mass.: Ballinger, 1974.

———, and Pejovich, Svetozar. "Property Rights and Economic Theory: A Survey of Recent Literature." *Journal of Economic Literature* 10 (December 1972): 1137–62.

Gardner, B. Delworth. "Transfer Restrictions and Misallocation in Grazing Public Range." *American Journal of Agricultural Economics* 49: 50–63.

Glasner, David. *Politics, Prices, and Petroleum. The Political Economy of Energy.* Cambridge, Mass.: Ballinger and Pacific Institute for Public Policy Research, 1983.

Gordon, H. Scott. "The Economic Theory of a Common Property Resource: The Fishery." *Journal of Political Economy* 62 (April 1954): 124–42.

———. "Economics and the Conservation Question." *Journal of Law and Economics* 1: 110–21.

Habicht, E. R., Jr. "Electric Utilities and Solar Energy: Competition, Subsidies, Ownership, and Prices." In *The Solar Market: Proceedings of the Symposium on Competition in the Solar Energy Industry.* Washington, D.C.: Federal Trade Commission, 1978.

Hall, George R. "The Myth and Reality of Multiple Use Forestry." *Natural Resources Journal* 3: 276–90.

Hallagan, William. "Share Contracting for California Gold." *Explorations in Economic History* 15 (April 1977): 196–210.

———. "Self-selection by Contracting Choice and the Theory of Sharecropping." *Bell Journal of Economics* 9 (Autumn 1978): 344–54.

Hansman, Jean M. "Urban Water Services Pricing: Public vs. Private Firms." Ph.D. thesis, Department of Economics, George Washington University, 1976.

Hardin, Garrett. "The Tragedy of the Commons." *Science* 162 (December 1968): 1243–48.

———, and Baden, John A. *Managing the Commons.* San Francisco: Freeman, 1977.

Hilton, George W. "The Consistency of the Interstate Commerce Act." *Journal of Law and Economics* 9 (October 1966): 87–113.

———. "The Basic Behavior of Regulatory Commissions." *American Economic Review* 62 (May 1972): 47–54.

Hirsch, Werner Z. "Cost Functions of Government Service: Refuse Collection." *Review of Economics and Statistics* 47 (February 1965): 87-92.

Hotelling, Harold. "The Economics of Exhaustible Resources." *Journal of Political Economy* 39 (April 1939).

Hyde, William F. *Timber Supply, Land Allocation, and Economic Efficiency.* Baltimore: Johns Hopkins Press, 1979.

Jackson, Raymond. "Regulation and Electric Utility Rate Levels." *Land Economics* 45 (August 1969): 372-76.

Jarrell, Gregg A. "The Demand for State Regulation of the Electric Utility Industry." *Journal of Law and Economics* 21 (October 1978): 269-96.

Jensen, Michael C., and Meckling, William H. "Theory of the Firm: Managerial Behavior, Agency Costs and Ownership Structure." *Journal of Financial Economics* 3 (October 1976): 305-60.

Johnson, M. Bruce, and Deacon, Robert, eds. *Forestlands: Public and Private.* Cambridge, Mass.: Ballinger and Pacific Institute for Public Policy Research, forthcoming.

Johnson, Ronald N., and Libecap, Gary D. "Redistribution Costs, Property Rights, and Resource Use: The Case of Southwestern Indian Reservations." February 1979. (Unpublished.)

_____. "Agency Costs and the Assignment of Property Rights: The Case of Southwestern Indian Reservations." *Southern Economic Journal* 47 (October 1980): 332-47.

_____. "Contracting Problems and Regulation: The Case of the Fishery." *American Economic Review*, December 1980.

_____. "Efficient Markets and Great Lakes Timber: A Conservation Issue Reexamined." *Explorations in Economic History*, October 1980.

Johnson, Ronald N.; Gisser, Micha; and Werner, Michael. "The Definition of a Surface Water Right and Transferability." *Journal of Law and Economics* 24 (October 1981): 273-88.

Jones, Derek C., and Backus, David K. "British Producer Cooperative in the Footwear Industry: An Empirical Evaluation of the Theory of Financing." *Economic Journal* 87 (September 1977): 488-510.

Jordan, William A. "Producer Perfection, Prior Market Structure and the Effects of Government Regulation." *Journal of Law and Economics* 15 (April 1972): 151-76.

Keeler, Theodore E. "Airline Regulation and Market Performance." *Bell Journal of Economics and Management Science* 3 (Autumn 1972): 399-424.

Kirzner, Israel. *Competition and Entrepreneurship.* Chicago: University of Chicago Press, 1973.

Klein, Benjamin; Crawford, Robert G.; and Alchian, Armen A. "Vertical Integration, Appropriate Rents, and the Competitive Contracting Process." *Journal of Law and Economics* 21 (October 1978): 297-326.

Krueger, Anne O. "The Political Economy of the Rent Seeking Society." *American Economic Review* 64 (June 1974): 291–303.

Larner, Robert J. "Ownership and Control in the 200 Largest Nonfinancial Corporations, 1929–1963." *American Economic Review* 56 (September 1966): 777–87.

Libecap, Gary D. "Economic Variables and the Development of Law: The Case of Western Mineral Rights." *Journal of Economic History* 38 (June 1978): 338–62.

_____ . "Bureaucratic Opposition to the Assignment of Property Rights: Overgrazing on the Western Range." *Journal of Economic History*, March 1980.

_____ . *Locking Up the Range: Federal Land Controls and Grazing.* Cambridge, Mass.: Ballinger and Pacific Institute for Public Policy Research, 1981.

_____ , and Johnson, Ronald N. "The Navajo and Too Many Sheep: Persistent Overgrazing on the Navajo Reservation." 1979. (Unpublished.)

_____ . "Legislating Commons: The Navajo Tribal Council and the Navajo Range." *Economic Inquiry* 87 (January 1980): 69–86.

Lindsay, Cotton M. "A Theory of Government Enterprise." *Journal of Political Economy* 87 (October 1976): 1061–77.

Maloney, M. T., and McCormick, R. E. "A Positive Theory of Environmental Quality Regulation." *Journal of Law and Economics*, April 1982.

Mancke, Richard B. "Competition and Monopoly in World Oil Markets: The Role of the International Oil Companies." *Cato Journal* 1 (1981): 107–27.

Mann, Patrick C. "Publicly Owned Electric Utility Profits and Resource Allocation." *Land Economics* 46 (November 1970): 478–84.

_____ , and Mikesell, John L. "Tax Payments and Electric Utility Prices." *Southern Economic Journal* 38 (July 1971): 69–78.

_____ , and Siefried, Edmond J. "Pricing in the Case of Publicly Owned Electric Utilities." *Quarterly Review of Economics and Business* 12 (Summer 1972): 77–89.

Manne, Henry G. "Mergers and the Market for Corporate Control." *Journal of Political Economy* 72 (April 1965): 110–20.

Martin, Donald L. "Job Property Rights and Job Defections." *Journal of Law and Economics* 15 (October 1972): 385–410.

_____ . "Some Economics of Job Rights in the Longshore Industry." *Journal of Economics and Business* 25 (Winter 1973): 93–100.

_____ . "The Economics of Employment Termination Rights." *Journal of Law and Economics* 20 (April 1977): 187–204.

McEachern, William A. "Corporate Control and Risk." *Economic Inquiry* 14 (June 1976): 270–78.

McKean, Roland. "Divergences between Individual and Total Cost within Government." *American Economic Review* 54 (May 1964): 243–49.

Meyer, Robert A. "Publicly Owned versus Privately Owned Utilities: A Policy Choice." *Review of Economics and Statistics* 17 (November 1975): 391–99.

Mikesell, John L. "Regulation and Electric Utility Rate Structure." *Mississippi Valley Journal of Economics and Business* 7 (Fall 1971): 82-89.

Mitchell, William. *The Anatomy of Government Failure.* Los Angeles: International Institute for Economic Research, 1979.

Moore, John H. *Worker Management and Industrial Growth in Yugoslavia.* Stanford, Calif.: Hoover Institution Press, 1980.

Moore, Thomas G. "The Effectiveness of Regulation of Electric Utility Prices." *Southern Economic Journal* 36 (April 1970): 365-75.

Moorhouse, John, ed. *Electric Utility Regulation and the Energy Crisis.* Cambridge, Mass.: Ballinger and Pacific Institute for Public Policy Research, forthcoming.

Nicols, Alfred. "Stock versus Mutual Savings and Loan Associations: Some Evidence of Differences in Behavior." *American Economic Review* 57 (May 1967): 337-47.

_____ . *Management and Control in the Mutual Savings and Loan Association.* Lexington, Mass.: Lexington Books, 1972.

Niskanen, William A. *Bureaucracy and Representative Government.* Chicago: Aldine, 1971.

_____ . "Bureaucracies and Politicians." *Journal of Law and Economics* 18 (1975): 617-43.

North, Douglass. "A Framework for Analyzing the State in Economic History." *Explorations in Economic History* 16 (1979): 249-59.

Oi, Walter Y. "Mutual Organizations: Comments." In *The Economics of Nonproprietary Organizations*, edited by Kenneth W. Clarkson and Donald L. Martin, pp. 104-9, Supplement to vol. 1, *Research in Law and Economics*, 1979.

Olson, Mancur, Jr. *The Logic of Collective Action.* New York: Schocken Books, 1965.

Ott, Mack. "Bureaucratic Incentives, Social Efficiency, and the Conflict in Federal Land Policy." *Cato Journal* 1 (Fall 1981): 585-607.

Pashigian, B. Peter. "Consequences and Causes of Public Ownership of Urban Transit Facilities." *Journal of Political Economy* 84 (December 1976): 1239-60.

Pejovich, Svetozar. *Fundamentals of Economics: A Property Rights Approach.* Dallas: The Fisher Institute, 1979.

Peltzman, Sam. "Pricing in Public and Private Enterprises: Electric Utilities in the United States." *Journal of Law and Economics* 14 (April 1971): 109-47.

_____ . "Toward a More General Theory of Regulation." *The Journal of Law and Economics* 19 (August 1976): 211-40.

Pike, John. "Residential Electric Rates and Regulation." *Quarterly Review of Economics and Business* 7 (Summer 1967): 45-52.

Pinchot, Gifford. *Breaking New Ground.* New York: Harcourt, Brace, 1947.

Posner, Richard A. "Taxation by Regulation." *Bell Journal of Economics and Management Science* 2 (Spring 1971): 22-50.

_____. *Economic Analysis of Law.* Boston: Little, Brown, 1972.

Primeaux, William J., Jr. "Rate Base Methods and Realized Rates of Return." *Economic Inquiry* 16 (January 1978): 95-107. (Originally titled, "The Rate Base as a Factor in Electric Utility Profits," this article was written in 1973.)

Public Land Law Review Commission. *One Third of the Nation's Land.* Washington, D.C.: Government Printing Office, 1970.

Robinson, Glen O. *The Forest Service.* Baltimore: Johns Hopkins Press, 1978.

Ruff, Larry E. "The Common Economic Sense of Pollution." *The Public Interest* 19 (Spring 1970): 69-85.

Rushing, William. "Differences in Profit and Nonprofit Organizations: A Study of Effectiveness and Efficiency in General Short-stay Hospitals." *Administration Science Quarterly* 19 (December 1974): 474-84.

Sav, George T. "R&D Decisions under Alternative Regulatory Constraints." *Atlantic Economic Journal* 5 (July 1977): 73-79.

Savas, E.S. "Policy Analysis for Local Government: Public vs. Private Refuse Collection." *Policy Analysis* 3 (Winter 1977): 49-74.

Schultze, C. *The Public Use of Private Interest.* Washington, D.C.: The Brookings Institution, 1977.

Scott, Anthony. "The Fishery: The Objectives of Sole Ownership." *Journal of Political Economy* 63 (April 1955): 116-24.

Shelton, John. "Allocative Efficiency v. 'X-Efficiency': Comment." *American Economic Review* 57 (December 1967): 1252-58.

Shepherd, William G. "Utility Growth and Profits under Regulation." In *Utility Regulation: New Directions in Theory and Practice*, edited by W.G. Shepherd and T.G. Gies. New York: Random House, 1966.

Siffin, William J. "Bureaucracy, Entrepreneurship, and Natural Resources: Witless Policy and the Barrier Islands." *Cato Journal* 1 (1981): 293-311.

Smith, Robert J. "Resolving the Tragedy of the Commons by Creating Private Property Rights in Wildlife." *Cato Journal* 1 (Fall 1981): 439-68.

Smith, Vernon L. "On Models of Commercial Fishing." *Journal of Political Economy* 77 (March/April 1969): 181-98.

_____. "The Primitive Hunter Culture." *Journal of Political Economy* 83 (August 1975): 727-56.

_____. "Water Deeds: A Proposed Solution to the Water Valuation Problem." *Arizona Review* 26 (January 1977): 7-10.

Spann, Robert M. "Rate of Return Regulation and Efficiency in Production: An Empirical Test of the Averch-Johnson Thesis." *Bell Journal of Economics and Management Science* 5 (Spring 1974): 38-52.

Stano, Miron. "Executive Ownership Interests and Corporate Performance." *Southern Economic Journal* 42 (October 1975): 272-78.

Steen, Harold K. *The Forest Service (1977): A History.* Seattle: University of Washington Press, 1977.

Stevens, Joe B., and Godfrey, E. Bruce. "Use Rates, Resource Flows, and Efficiency of Public Investment in Range Improvements." *American Journal of Agricultural Economics* 54 (November 1972): 611-21.

Stigler, George J. "The Theory of Economic Regulation." *Bell Journal of Economics and Management Science* 2 (Spring 1971): 3-21.

_____, and Friedland, Claire. "What Can Regulators Regulate? The Case of Electricity." *Journal of Law and Economics* 5 (October 1962): 1-16.

Theroux, David J., and Truluck, Phillip N., eds. *Private Rights and Public Lands.* Washington, D.C.: Co-published by the Pacific Institute for Public Policy Research and Heritage Foundation, 1982.

Tilton, John E. "The Nature of Firm Ownership and the Adoption of Innovations in the Electric Power Industry." Paper presented at the meetings of the Public Choice Society, Washington, D.C., March 1973.

Trosper, Ronald L. "American Indian Relative Ranching Efficiency." *American Economic Review* 68 (September 1978): 503-16.

Tullock, Gordon. *The Politics of Bureaucracy.* Washington, D.C.: Public Affairs Press, 1965.

_____. *Private Wants and Public Means.* New York: Basic Books, 1970.

_____. "The Cost of Transfers." *Kyklos* 24 (1971): 629-43.

Umbeck, John. "A Theory of Contract Choice and the California Gold Rush." *Journal of Law and Economics* 20 (October 1977): 421-37.

Vale, Thomas R. "Presettlement Vegetation in the Sagebrush-Grass Area of the Intermountain West." *Journal of Range Management* 28 (January 1975): 32-36.

Villajero, Don. "Stock Ownership and the Control of Corporations." *University Thought* 2 (Autumn 1961): 33-77 and 3 (Winter 1962): 47-65.

Voigt, William, Jr. *Public Grazing Lands.* New Brunswick, N.J.: Rutgers University Press, 1976.

Weidenbaum, M. L., and Harnish, R. *Government Credit Subsidies for Energy Development.* Washington, D.C.: American Enterprise Institute, 1976.

Wildavsky, Aaron. *The Politics of the Budgetary Process.* Boston: Little, Brown, 1964.

Williamson, Oliver E. *The Economics of Discretionary Behavior: Managerial Objectives in a Theory of the Firm.* Englewood Cliffs, N.J.: Prentice-Hall, 1964.

Wilson, George W., and Jadlow, Joseph M. "Competition, Profit Incentives, and Technical Efficiency in the Nuclear Medicine Industry." 1978. (Unpublished.)

Yandle, Bruce. "The Emerging Market for Air Pollution Rights." *Regulation*, July-August 1978, pp. 21-29.

Zerbe, Richard O., Jr. "The Costs and Benefits of Early Regulation of the Railroads." *Bell Journal of Economics* 11 (1980).

INDEX

alternative, 59–66 *passim*
innovation in, 58–59
regulation of, 56–57, 67
subsidies to, 59–66
Energy, Department of, 57
Environmentalists. *See also*
Conservation movement
and forest management, 117
and pollution control, 93–94
private land management by,
109–110
and the Sagebrush Rebellion, 102,
103–104, 105, 107
Environmental Protection Agency
(EPA), 90–93 *passim*, 96
Environmental quality. *See also*
Pollution
and cultural values, 37
and institutional design, 37–38
and timber production, 112
Equity
in market system, 16, 21
in pollution control, 88–89, 95, 97
Eskimo, the, 32, 53
Externalities, 18–19
of buffalo harvest, 34
of bureaucratic management, 45–49
passim
and the commons, 41
of forest management, 124
of groundwater use, 70–71, 72, 73

Federalist Papers, 27
Federal Power Commission (FPC), 42,
56, 66
Fishing, 86
Florida, 70
Flow resource, 71, 80–81
Forests
harvesting of, 45
management of, 104, 105, 114–118
mismanagement of, 102
private ownership of, 118–119, 123,
124–125
productivity of, 111–112
public ownership of, 116
sale of, 122, 123–126
value of, 113–114, 115, 125–126
Forest Service, 44, 113, 118, 126
management practices of, 114,
115–116
mismanagement by, 102

and pinyon-juniper chaining, 48–49
structure of, 105
and timber production, 45, 111–112
French fur traders, 35, 36
Frontier, American
closing of, 13–14
economic development of, 10–13
Fur trade, 35–36

Gas, natural, 65, 66
in private wildlife sanctuary, 50
regulation of, 42, 56
Gasahol, 60
Germany, 121
Government. *See* Bureaucratic
behavior; Bureaucratic management; Politics
Grazing lands, 46, 47, 48–49, 102
Groundwater
allocation of, 75–83
central management of, 79–80
as common pool resource, 70–73
laws governing, 73–78
recharge, overdraft of, 71–73, 72n
supplies of, 70

Haines, Francis, 33 and n. 5
Hardin, Garrett, 42
Hayek, Friedrich A., 104, 117
Health, Education, and Welfare,
Department of, 90
Homestead Act of 1862, 12–13
Hydroelectric power, 58, 59, 64–65
Hydrologic studies, 81

Idaho, 106
Incentives, 4–5, 30
and environmental quality, 37, 38
and frontier development, 10–11
of groundwater allocation, 82–83
and price information, 115
Information, 30
in bureaucratic management, 44–45,
79
in changing environments, 105
and decisionmaking, 5, 44–45
in forest management, 114–118
passim
in groundwater management, 79, 81,
82
in pollution control, 89, 92

ABOUT THE AUTHORS

Richard L. Stroup is professor of agricultural economics and economics and co-director of the Center for Political Economy and Natural Resources at Montana State University. He received his B.A., M.A., and Ph.D. from the University of Washington, and is presently serving as Director, Office of Policy Analysis, U.S. Department of the Interior.

Dr. Stroup has taught economics at the University of Washington (1966–68) and Seattle University (1969), and was Visiting Associate Professor of Economics, Florida State University (1974, 1979).

He is the author of *Economics: Private and Public Choice* (with J. Gwartney) and the editor of *Bureaucracy vs. Environment* (with J. Baden). A contributor to many scholarly volumes, his articles have appeared in *Cato Journal, Economic Inquiry, Journal of Law and Economics, Literature of Liberty, Montana Business Quarterly, Policy Review, Public Choice, Reason, Southern Economic Journal*, and other journals.

John A. Baden is director of the Center for Political Economy and Natural Resources at Montana State University. He received his B.A. from Wittenberg University and his Ph.D. from Indiana University, and has been on the faculty at Indiana University, Utah State University, University of Oregon, Oregon State University, and the University of Texas at Dallas.

147

He is the editor of *Managing the Commons* (with G. Hardin), *Bureaucracy vs. Environment* (with R. L. Stroup), and *Earth Day Reconsidered.* He has also been the guest editor of several journals. Dr. Baden's articles have appeared in *Cato Journal, Economic Inquiry, Environmental Education, Environmental Law, Journal of Law and Economics, Literature of Liberty, Policy Report, Policy Review, Public Choice, Reason, Western Wildlands,* and other popular and scholarly journals.

He has also been a contract logger and timber buyer. He and his wife, Ramona Marotz-Baden, own and manage a family ranch in the Gallatin Valley of Montana.